The Race for
Good Credit

HOW TO ESTABLISH, MAINTAIN, AND WIN WITH GOOD CREDIT

Trent L. Pettus

Trent L. Pettus/The Race for Good Credit
Printed in the United States of America

The Race for Good Credit/ Trent L. Pettus -- 1st ed.

ISBN 978-0-692-87691-6 Print Edition
ISBN 978-0-692-87692-3 Ebook Edition

Contents

Acknowledgments

To all of my family and friends who supported me during this special project, and encouraged me to continue to reach as many people as possible so their financial futures may be changed forever.

Forward

At last an informational, delicately crafted, detailed, yet interesting book on CREDIT! The Race for Good Credit is destined to find its way into personal libraries and onto desks, laptops, night-tables, and briefcases, of people across the country. I assure you, it will quickly earn a top spot as the go-to, step-by-step guide to the dilemmas and joys of Good CREDIT.

As I thumbed through the pages, I instantly began to wonder where this book was when I was first starting out in the adult world, as a young parent raising children, and well beyond. I thought about the family meetings or reunions I could have had to discuss the serious aspects of CREDIT, thereby saving people I cared about from many situations that negatively impacted their lives for years to come.

Here is just a taste of what you can expect from the following pages:

- Learn what Credit Reports and Credit Scores are all about
- Identity Theft—how to avoid it and what to do if it happens to you
- Married, Divorce and your credit
- Repairing your Credit
- AND MORE......MUCH, MUCH MORE

Has your appetite been sparked? Congratulations in advance for making the decision to read and study this book. You will enhance your financial literacy, thereby shifting your life's trajectory toward present and future success.

I say with a smile, a big "Thank You" to Trent, for extending his gift of understanding the world of CREDIT.

It is never too late to improve your credit no matter what stage of life you're in. We're all in this race! You still have a chance to win especially now that you have this book! The Race for Good Credit is on! Ready...Get set...Go!

Submitted by

Lucille W. Ijoy, Ed.D.

Executive Director, Motivation Institute of Philadelphia

Introduction

We are blessed to live in a society full of bright, shiny objects of desire. Unfortunately, as a result, it's easy to get caught up in the race to acquire all the things we want. In so many cases, we have far too easy access to that "performance-enhancing drug" known as credit.

Some of us have even overdosed.

With my first introduction to credit, I nearly disqualified myself from the race. I was in college some thirty years ago, and the credit card companies had tables set up at the student union. All you had to do was fill out an application and show your student ID to prove that you were enrolled as at least a sophomore. A few weeks later, a shiny plastic card with your name on it showed up in the mail.

In a matter of a few weeks, I was able to acquire even more credit cards. Six of them, to be exact. No proof of income or the ability to pay the bill each month was even necessary. The only requirement was that you were a student, never mind a struggling one, at that.

As a full-time student, waiting tables part-time, I had barely enough to buy food and pay the utility bills, much less window-shop at the local mall. Suddenly, with several new shiny credit cards, each with at least a $500 limit, I was literally in the money.

Or was I?

A few months, and far too many unnecessary purchases later, I was also in major debt. I could not pay the minimum on the bills when I received the statements, and American Express even expected payment in full at the end of each month. Seeing as I had to pay rent, buy food, and pay my utility payments before I could think about paying my credit cards, I did what most nineteen--or twenty-year-olds with no idea what they were supposed to do would do. That is to say, I simply ignored the problem and did nothing at all. The next thing I knew, my accounts went into collection, and my credit, a concept I didn't fully understand, was ruined.

Up until that time, I had always been a good student and a responsible young man, but I knew nothing about credit, credit scores, or the impact of not making the monthly payments in a timely manner. I didn't even realize I was engaging in totally irresponsible behavior. As a result, the negative consequences of my actions haunted me for years to come.

The experience definitely impacted the start of my adult life. Little did I know, the concept and reality of credit would also define my future.

A week after I graduated from college, I moved to Boston and began to work at a real estate firm. I didn't have a clue what a mortgage was, much less a deed or any other real estate documents or concepts. I like to think I'm a quick study, and it seems the industry suited my intellectual curiosity. Over the years, I found myself working in various areas of the real estate industry, including commercial and residential sales, property management, as a mortgage broker, as a housing and credit counselor, in commercial and real estate development, and eventually as the host of "Let's Talk Real Estate" on a local radio show in Philadelphia. In September of 2010, I opened Integrity Real Estate Services, a full-service real estate brokerage, licensed in Pennsylvania and Delaware. Recently, I also began teaching real estate classes at a local real estate school.

Very quickly in the process of working my way up and around the world of real estate, I came to realize just how important the whole concept (and reality) of good credit really is. Everyone needs good credit—from students starting out, to senior citizens looking to refinance a home they've owned for decades. As a result, I developed a true and enduring passion for teaching people about the importance of credit. I'll read anything on the subject and find it thoroughly fascinating, particularly after working three years as a housing and credit counselor at a nonprofit counseling agency. The agency was set up to help people become homeowners, help them with their credit issues, and help them if they were having problems paying their mortgages. I conducted a lot of the first-time homebuyer and credit workshops and seminars, and I did a lot of credit counseling. It was easily the most rewarding and impactful work I've ever done in the industry.

Many of the people who came into the agency seemed to have two things in common: they either had bad credit or did not know that it was bad. Few had ever looked at their credit reports. Most didn't even know that along with their own financial missteps, or their desire for those bright shiny objects, they also had errors on their credit reports that, if corrected, would significantly raise their credit scores and enable them to qualify for mortgages or other forms of credit at lower rates of interest. Later, as a real estate broker, I would send people to get pre-approved for mortgages, only to have the lenders pull their reports and reject them because their credit scores were too low—sometimes because of incorrect, incomplete, or outdated information on their credit reports.

I often found myself with the not-so-great job of breaking the news that they'd have to dispute these items and that it was going to take months before they would be able to get that house they wanted. That was, assuming someone else hadn't already snapped it up. Worse, sometimes the primary breadwinner in a family had bad credit despite having a good income and the ability to afford the monthly payments, and could not qualify for the loan because his or her credit score was below the minimum to qualify.

After reviewing literally thousands of credit reports and seeing the sometimes heart-breaking consequences of bad credit, I've become painfully aware of how many uninformed people are out there and how much misinformation we all have to deal with. I also began to realize how easily this distress could be avoided. This, I am sure, only served to fuel my passion about the subject.

While some may call me a credit geek, I prefer to think of myself as a coach on a mission to help teach people what to do to establish, clean up, maintain, and increase their credit scores. We've all had our missteps and our stumbles, but fear not. With me as your coach, there will be no hiding, or, worse, quitting. If you want to understand your credit and how to improve it, then I will show you how to train for the most important race you will ever run. You may get weary, you may get tired, but there's no reason to quit the Race for Good Credit. If you finish strong there will be rewards—low interest rates on cars and credit cards, the ability to qualify for a loan to purchase a home, and countless other benefits.

Ready? Get set. Let's go!

CHAPTER ONE

Getting in Shape for the Race
Test Your Credit Knowledge

For his eighteenth birthday, I made my godson apply for a credit card. Yes, a credit card.

Now, before you ask, *what kind of present is that,* hear me out.

"My gift to you is that we will build your credit together, the right way, from the start," I told him. I also gave him the following instructions, which he promised he'd follow to the letter: "You will use this credit card once, on the birthday present of your choice. The card is in your name, but I will pay the bill. I am going to pay off the gift, on time, every month for the next six months, to make sure you establish a good credit score."

I also instructed him to open a savings account and save for a home—which is exactly what he did.

For the next few years, we built his credit together and he saved money. At the age of 21, his credit was good enough to purchase his first house—a beautifully rehabbed home in the northeast section of Philadelphia.

A couple of years later, I gave him a car.

Yes, as you can probably imagine, my godson is extremely important to me, but no, I'm not the slightest bit insane. I definitely DID NOT run down to the dealership and put a car in his name, or, heaven forbid, co-sign on a loan. Not even close. What I did do was give him my high-mileage, good condition, 1995 Mercedes that I rarely drove. It was a win-win for all. He got a vehicle in good condition, and I got the satisfaction of knowing he would be driving a safe car.

More important, I sent my godson into adulthood with a good credit score and no inclination to rush into a luxury purchase that so many people make long before they can truly afford to do so.

My godson will tell you that understanding credit was an integral part of his upbringing and, now, his successful future. While I wish I could do for everyone what I did for my godson, the one gift that I can give is to share the information I've learned with others so they too can develop, maintain, and increase their credit scores.

If you take nothing else out of this book, remember this: YOUR CREDIT SCORE IS CRUCIALLY IMPORTANT, and you must do everything you can to build and keep it as high as possible!

Why is a good credit score so critically important?

In this book, I'll be explaining, in as simple a format as possible, why good credit matters and what you can do to change bad habits, develop good habits, and maintain your new habits for the long haul. Before I launch into my pre-race pep talk, however, let me start things off with a few examples:

William saw an ad for zero percent financing on a car he'd been dreaming of for years. He rushed down to the car dealership, fully intending to buy on the spot. That was, until he found out his credit score was 510. After hours of waiting, and a whole lot of stress, he was finally offered a loan for a car with an interest rate that was not only far from zero percent, but also well into the double digits. As a result of his damaged credit, the monthly payment made the car completely out of his reach. In fact, it made any new car all but impossible until he could repair his credit and increase his credit score.

＊

George and Elena fell in love. After a whirlwind courtship, they got engaged and set a date to be married. George made a good income, Elena about a third less, but together they had a sizeable down payment and could easily afford a single-family home in a neighborhood with award-winning schools. Everything was coming up roses for the young couple until they started shopping for a mortgage. Elena had a credit score of close to 800. Unfortunately, George had made a few mistakes and had more than a few negative marks on his credit report. His score was 545. As a result, the couple, who hadn't given any thought to discussing their separate financial situations before coming together, could only qualify for a house in her name because his credit score was too low. Worse, that also meant only her income would be considered and their housing choices were now limited to properties that she could qualify for alone. They went from looking at single-style homes in an ideal part of town to smaller townhomes in a much less desirable neighborhood.

＊

Miles went through three rounds of interviews for a position at the airport that matched his skill set to a T, or so said the manager who conducted the final meeting. The job was his, and he was scheduled to start at the beginning of the month. The only formality was a credit check by his new employer, which he readily signed off on. While he hadn't exactly been diligent about paying bills on time, had a car repossessed once, and his unpaid credit card ended up with a collection company, he was more surprised than anyone when he got a call a few days later saying that the company was going to have to go with their second-choice candidate because of unfavorable information on his credit report.

What does it all mean?

After thirty years in the real estate business, including an extended stint as a housing and credit counselor at a nonprofit counseling agency, I've helped countless people clean up their credit in the aftermath of sometimes heart-breaking financial scenarios. While this credit bureau stuff may sometimes seem like unfair mumbo-jumbo, the fact of the matter is that if somebody looks at your credit report and it isn't as clean as it should be, you may not be able to get a credit card, much less a car, or qualify for a mortgage. If you are able to qualify for loans with mediocre credit, the interest rate and the monthly payment alone may make the purchase out of the question.

And yes, good credit is not only important, but also sometimes imperative, for potential employment in all but a handful of cities and states.

How credit fit are you?

My real estate office is located in Mount Airy, a racially and culturally diverse community in Philadelphia. The average house we sell is probably around $150,000, and the majority of our buyers are first-time homebuyers. Most of our clients are African Americans, and a large percentage of them are single women with children. Every day, people call or come into our office wanting to become first-time homebuyers. Unfortunately, as soon as we refer them to loan officers for pre-approvals, too many of them get denied because of past credit issues. Why? I've found that even the most savvy folks have misinformation and confusion on the subject of credit. In fact, the bulk of people I've asked do not have any idea what their current credit score is unless they've recently tried to make a large purchase that involved financing. I have been conducting first-time homebuyer and credit seminars for years in a variety of different communities. The one commonality I've found, no matter where I'm speaking, is that credit confusion, as I like to call it, is prevalent amongst people of every demographic and income level.

People of all ages and economic circumstances find their lives adversely impacted as a result of their credit scores. To test their knowledge about the ins and outs of credit, I created a credit quiz that I use at my seminars and would like for you to take now:

Test your credit knowledge

Answer the following questions and we'll see if you're credit fit or a little flabbier than you might have realized:

1. The highest FICO® credit score is 950.
True or False?

2. In order to generate a credit score, I need at least one credit account that has been open for 6 months or longer.
True or False?

3. A low credit score can keep me from getting a certain job or promotion.
True or False?

4. My payment history affects my credit score more than any other factor.
True or False?

5. Co-signing for family and friends is usually a bad idea.
True or False?

6. A credit repair company can <u>legally</u> remove negative information from my credit report that is accurate.
True or False?

7. The 3 major credit bureaus are Equifax, Experian, and TransUnited.
True or False?

8. The only site where I can get a free report each year as mandated by the federal government is www.freecreditreport.com.
True or False?

9. The Fair Credit Reporting Act (FCRA) is designed to help ensure that all information in my credit file is complete, accurate, and not outdated. ?
True or False?

10. I should review my credit report at least once a year.
True or False?

11. Race, gender, and employment history are factored into my credit score.
True or False?

12. Negative information remains on my credit report for 7 years from the date of the missed payment that led to the delinquency.
True or False?

13. A collection account can be reported for 7 additional years if sold to a different collection agency.
True or False?

14. All judgments, whether paid or unpaid, remain on my credit report for 10 years from the date filed.
True or False?

15. Unpaid tax liens can remain on my credit report indefinitely.
True or False?

16. Chapter 7, 11 and 12 bankruptcies can remain on my credit report for 10 years from the date filed; Chapter 13 bankruptcies can remain for 7 years from the date paid.
True or False?

17. A 30-day late payment made today is not as bad as a 180-day late payment made 6 years ago.
True or False?

18. When I get my credit card balances to zero, I should close them.

True or False?

19. If I apply for credit cards at Macy's and The Gap today, my score will drop two times.

True or False?

20. All auto, student loan, mortgage-related inquiries made within 30 days of scoring are completely ignored.

True or False?

21. Identity theft is one of the fastest-growing crimes in the country.

True or False?

22. According to a recent FTC study, 20% of all credit reports contain mistakes.

True or False?

23. Credit Scoring is a risk-based system creditors use to determine whether to give me credit.

True or False?

24. There is a strong correlation between a low credit score and poor job performance

True or False?

25. Carrying high student-loan debt will hurt my credit score.

True or False?

Score your answers:

1: False, 2: True, 3: True, 4: True, 5: True, 6: False, 7: False, 8: False, 9: True, 10: True, 11: False, 12: True, 13: False, 14: False, 15: True, 16: True, 17: False, 18: False, 19: True, 20: True, 21: True, 22: True, 23: True, 24: False, 25: False

How did you do?

20-25 Correct Answers: You are already winning the race with your knowledge—keep running, the race is not over until you get to the end.

15-19 Correct Answers: You are maintaining a steady pace, a pace that will enable you to finish the race.

10-14 Correct Answers: If you train a little harder you could run a good race.

Less than 10 Correct Answers: Let's start from the beginning.

Did you do better than you expected? Much worse? If so, don't despair. As I've mentioned, most people don't have more than a general awareness that they have a credit score, much less what it is and why it's important. I developed this quiz for my credit seminars and have been amazed by how many people get many of the answers wrong. By the end of the seminars, the participants have gained lots of knowledge about credit and credit scores.

And knowledge is power.

To that end, let's discuss a few of the questions directly addressed in this chapter. Answers to the rest of the questions, as well as many others, will be discussed throughout the book.

Question: The highest FICO® score or credit score is 950. True or False?

Answer: False

The highest FICO® score is 850. It is nearly impossible to achieve this score. To do so, a person must pay his bills on time, keep low balances on his credit cards, and not apply for a lot of new credit in a short period of time. A good score is fairly easy to earn if you follow the guidelines we'll be discussing throughout the book. A credit score over 780 will result in preferred rates on everything from credit cards to mortgages. As a point of reference, the median credit score in the country is 690. That is according to FICO® or Fair Isaac Corporation, the company that developed the scoring model. FICO® is the most widely used scoring system in the United States.

Question: In order to generate a credit score, I need at least one credit account that has been open for 6 months or longer.
True or False?

    Answer: True

The best way to establish a credit score is to go down to your local bank or credit union and apply for a secured credit card in your name. A secured credit card is a type of credit card that is backed by a savings account used as collateral on the credit available with the card. The limit is based on previous credit history (if you have any) and the amount deposited in the account. If you pay every month on time, for six months, you will have established a history of paying your debts in a timely fashion, and thus establish yourself as someone worthy of being issued higher-limit unsecured credit. Make sure the credit card companies report your payment history to the credit bureaus each month.

Question: A low credit score can keep me from getting a certain job or promotion.
True or False?

    Answer: True

According to the Society of Human Resource Management, "The number of employers who conducted pre-employment credit checks is on the rise, up from 36 percent to 43 percent."

Many employers run credit to determine whether they are going to hire or promote you. While there is a lot of controversy around this practice, and the Equal Employment Opportunity Commission (EEOC) wants to eliminate the use of employers excluding applicants based on their criminal background, it is currently legal.

Contrary to popular perception, employers are not looking at your actual credit score, but how you pay your bills. They want to see if there are bankruptcies, tax liens, judgments, late payments, and the like. By law, they can't look at your actual score, and they are definitely not getting all your personal information, but potential creditors and employers can see if you've been engaged in criminal activity.

While there's never been a proven correlation between a low credit score and poor job performance, and there are many legitimate reasons why someone's credit can be compromised (a layoff or divorce, for example), the key is knowing what's on that report and what needs to be done to make sure it looks as sparkling as your resume.

We're all in this together

If you're reading this book because you're new to the whole concept of credit or are trying to do everything you can to maintain your credit, keep reading. If you're reading because you've made missteps, however serious, I'm here to help. My first mistake, ruining my credit at a young age with too many credit cards I couldn't pay, certainly wasn't my last. I learned about bad credit and the dangers of debt the hard way, too. I can't promise that learning how to manage and retrain bad habits will be easy. There will be sacrifices, both expected and surprising. I can promise you are not on this path alone.

Before we move on to Chapter Two, where we'll start your *Basic Training*, I want to share one more story that highlights just how easy it is for any of us to trip up in the middle of the race.

A well-dressed client came into my office. He was in his forties and drove a Mercedes. His wife had a BMW. He happened to be the cousin of the receptionist, so no one was more surprised than her when he showed up. After all, he was considered the "rich one" in her extended family. He and his wife had a big house outside of Philadelphia try. They were both college graduates. They had a timeshare in Aruba. They had children in private schools.

As it turned out, this couple both made good money, but there were large student loans and tons of other obligations. They were paying out more than what they were bringing in. So much so, that this gentleman came into my office on the verge of filing bankruptcy and wondering what to do.

I looked over all of his assets and suggested that he start by getting rid of the timeshare and at least one of their luxury cars (along with the car note).

His response?

"What will people think? I can't get rid of my nice cars and a lot of things I have because everyone thinks that we have a lot."

"I'll let you in on a secret," I said. "You don't."

"I know," he said. "But—"

"But if you bring in $175,000 and you spend $185,000, that means you're $10,000 in the hole," I continued. "You've created all this stress for yourself because you're trying to impress some folks who really don't care. Not enough for you to lose everything over their opinion of what they think you have, anyway."

In this situation, the client and his wife discussed what I'd said, and I proceeded to help them do what had to be done to get their spending back in line with their income. They made sacrifices which included trading in the cars, and getting over the idea that they needed the newest and the best every year just for appearances' sake. The takeaway for this couple, and hopefully for those of you reading this book, is that while many of us live to impress others, it's ultimately more important that we are impressed with ourselves.

Doesn't a good, healthy credit score do both?

CHAPTER TWO

Basic Training

Credit Reports

Whether you are brand new to the concept of credit, have had major issues, or are somewhere in between, knowledge is not only power, it's fuel for the race. The more you understand about how credit works, the more techniques you'll have at your disposal for winning the credit race.

My youngest brother walked into a car dealership, was shown cars, picked the model he wanted, and began to negotiate. By negotiate, I mean he asked for the low interest rate he'd seen advertised for "select consumers." The salesman gave him a practiced "yeah, right" look, and went to pull his credit. The next thing he knew, my brother, who has a nearly perfect credit score because he has never paid a bill late, nor made any of the mistakes nearly everyone else has made at some point or another, was signing paperwork for the car he wanted at exactly the terms he expected.

Just the way a good report card helps get you into college or snag a job, a good credit report can help you get things you want on the terms you want, be it a mortgage, credit card, personal loan, apartment, automobile, or even that plum job. Because good credit is such a valuable financial tool, you'll want to protect yours so it's there for you when you need it. In this section, we'll talk about everything you need to know to understand credit bureaus, what they do, and what you can do to make sure your credit report is as clean and accurate as it can be.

Ready?

What are Credit Bureaus?

Credit bureaus, also known as credit reporting companies, are in the business of collecting, packaging, and selling information about your financial life to lenders, employers, insurance agencies, and other customers. There are three major credit-reporting agencies. Combined, they collect and report more than 4.5 billion pieces of credit-related information each month. The credit bureau maintains the information it collects on you in a credit record or file, which is actually a history of your use and management of credit.

Question: The three major credit bureaus are Equifax, Expedia and TransUnited.
True or False?
Answer: False

The three major credit bureaus are Equifax, Expedia and **TransUnion.**

Some credit card lenders get a credit score from only one of the three big credit-reporting firms. Mortgage lenders, however, typically pull FICO® scores from all three firms. Your scores will be very similar, but not exactly the same from one credit report to the next.

What's in a credit report?

If you thought you got the last report card of your life when you graduated from school, think again. Credit reports continually keep track and grade you on how you pay your bills. A credit report includes information on where you live, how you pay your bills, whether you've been sued, arrested, or have filed for bankruptcy. Credit bureaus sell the information in your report to creditors, insurers, employers, and other businesses that use it to evaluate your applications for credit, insurance, employment, and rental properties.

There are a number of sections to every credit report and a lot of numbers, abbreviations, and terms you've probably never seen, nor thought about before.

There are four main sections in a credit report:

1. Header/Identifying Information

The **Header** contains your name and any other names you've previously used, current and former addresses, your Social Security number, date of birth, current and previous employers.

2. Credit History

The **Credit History** lists the accounts in your name reported by creditors, such as mortgage lenders, auto finance companies, and credit card issuers. Creditors that furnish information generally report the type of credit (auto loan, mortgage loan, credit card), the credit limit of the loan amount, account balance, the account payment history, including the timeliness of the payments, whether any accounts are in collection, and the dates the account was opened and closed. It includes accounts or loans you have open, outstanding balances, credit limits, and payment history. These individual accounts can also be called "trade lines."

On some reports, your credit history may be described in terms such as "never pays late," "typically pays thirty days late," *or* is "charged off"—which means the creditor has tried to collect from you, but has given up. Other agencies use payment codes ranging from one to nine. The lower the number, the better your rating.

Question: Negative information remains on my credit report for 7 years from the date of a missed payment that led to a delinquency. True or False?

Answer: True

Any derogatory information that is added to your credit report will remain for seven years. That negative information remains on your credit report for seven years from the date of a missed payment that led to a delinquency. Those who furnish the information to the credit bureaus must provide the month and year of the delinquency to the credit bureau in order to determine when the seven-year period ends. This information must be provided to the credit bureau within ninety days from the date the item is furnished to the credit bureau.

Public Record Information includes bankruptcies, judgments, and state and federal tax liens. Any information that appears in this section of your credit report will have a negative impact on your scores. Ideally, you want the **Public Record Information** section of your credit report to be blank. Not included in your credit report is specific information about your medical history, buying habits, or your bank account information.

Chapter 13 bankruptcies also remain on your credit history for seven years, but from the date they were paid. Chapter 7, 11 and 12 bankruptcies can stay on your credit report for ten years from the date they were filed, whether paid or not. The bottom line is, nothing hurts your credit score more than a bankruptcy; your credit score could potentially drop 200-300 points. Filing for bankruptcy protection should be your last resort after you've researched all other options.

Judgments

Question: All judgments, whether paid or unpaid, remain on my credit report for 10 years from the date filed.
True or False?

Answer: False

Judgments remain on your credit history for seven years from the day they are **filed,** not **paid**. That's the key. Get a judgment at 20 and you'll be 27 before you can get a mortgage to purchase a home. What if you get married in that time and want to buy a car or need a small personal loan? You want to do your best to avoid making mistakes that will affect you for such a long time. Judgments should be avoided at all costs.

Question: Unpaid tax liens can remain on my credit report indefinitely.
True or False?

Answer: True

Nothing stays on your credit report longer. They are usually removed after about fifteen years, but they can remain indefinitely. If you have a tax lien, view it as a priority—pay it in full or make payment arrangements as soon as you can. Now, the IRS will withdraw a tax lien if you pay it in full or enter into an installment agreement that will eventually result in full payment. Afterwards, you can request a withdrawal be filed, which can be done using IRS Form 12277.

3. Inquiries

The **Inquiries** section of your credit report lists everyone who has asked to see your credit report in the past two years for employment purposes, and for at least the last year for credit uses and most non-employment uses (i.e. tenant screening, insurance, government licenses or benefits). If you are denied credit, the lender must give you the name, address, and telephone number of the company that provided the report, and you'll see them listed here.

The important thing to know about this section is that every time you apply for credit and your credit is pulled, your credit score drops; however, there are exceptions and those exceptions will be covered. For your information, there are two types of inquiries you should be aware of: soft inquiries and hard inquiries.

Soft Inquiries:

Also known as Involuntary Checks, **Soft Inquiries** come from credit card companies who want to send you pre-approved credit cards, an employer who runs your credit, or from your current creditors who may be monitoring your account. They **do not** affect your credit score unless you accept the credit card offer, at which time the inquiry becomes a hard inquiry and your score will be affected. No one else sees those but you, so if you go to apply for an increase in your card limit, you would know that the credit card company pulled it to see if they wanted to give you an increase, and only you would see that pull on your report. The main thing to remember is this: you're not actually applying for credit. Someone is just looking at it for whatever reason and your credit rating is unaffected by these inquiries.

Hard Inquiries:

Also known as Voluntary Credit Checks, **Hard Inquiries** are ones you initiate by filling out a credit application. So, if you go to five different department stores today and apply for their credit cards, your score is going to drop five different times and it could be about three to five points each time.

Question: Inquiries remain on your credit report for seven years. True or False?
Answer: False

Inquiries can remain on your credit report for two years, but they're not factored in your score after the first year.

Question: My employer can get my credit report.
True or False?
    Answer: True

Your employer can get a copy of your credit report, but only if you agree. A credit bureau may not provide information about you to your employer, or to a prospective employer, without your written consent. Note that a credit report pulled by an employer will not have a credit score.

4.FICO® score

All the above information combined adds up to your FICO® score. Your FICO® score is a credit score developed by Fair Isaac Corporation to determine the likelihood that you, as a credit user, will pay your bills. FICO® scores range from 300 to 850 and have a significant impact on your ability to get loans and other credit, and the interest rate you'll receive to do so. FICO® scores are used in 90% of consumer-lending decisions, according to CEB TowerGroup, a financial services research firm.

Knowing and keeping track of your FICO® scores will give you a good indication of whether you are likely to get approved for a new loan, and whether it will be a good rate. If your score is low, knowing your current score is a good starting point for getting your credit back in order. Additionally, a sudden dive in your FICO® score could be a warning that someone has fraudulently opened accounts in your name. Because your FICO® score is calculated using the information contained in your credit report, anything inaccurate, incorrect, or obsolete can hurt your score.

Understanding FICO® and other credit scores

Credit scoring is a way for lenders to predict statistically how risky it is to lend money to someone. There are actually many different credit scores, but FICO® (which is not only a score type, but a brand) is the most widely used. FICO® builds a large number of scoring systems, like bankruptcy scores, fraud scores and industry-specific variations of their FICO® Credit Risk. You may have heard of VantageScore, which was developed by the three major credit bureaus to compete with FICO®. Again, 90% of lenders use FICO® scores in their lending decisions. In this book, we are focused only on FICO® and their credit bureau-based risk scores.

Not to confuse the issue, but there are different variations or generations of credit scores out there, depending on whether you are buying a car, getting a personal loan, getting insurance, or buying a house. There are different factors that each of the companies looks at. Basically your score is going to be your score with some variation from one to the other, based on certain factors they are looking for.

A credit score can be thought of almost like a cell phone. Every cell phone makes phone calls, but each one has different features. Your basic FICO® score is like a cell phone. It tells the creditor whether or not you are likely to default on a certain credit obligation within the next two years. The more specific scores are tailored to a certain industry. For example, a car dealership will want to know the likelihood of you paying your car loan. They are going to look at things like did you have a car loan before? Have you ever had a repossession? Did you pay your car off? If they are going to give you a car, they want to know more about your car paying habits than your mortgage paying habits. If you've had ten cars and you've never paid late, they won't care very much what you did with Sears or the mortgage company. The FICO® score they are interested in may well be different because they are putting more emphasis on your past payments with your cars. This industry-specific FICO® score is known as an Auto Score.

For this reason, each of the three credit bureaus has six or seven FICO® scores per scoreable consumer that collectively account for over 90% of the FICO® scores that were pulled in the past year. In most cases, all of a consumer's FICO® scores should be in the same ballpark, and generally don't vary by more than 25 points.

In the end, all the FICO® scores do one thing: they determine the likelihood that you will become ninety days or more delinquent on a credit obligation within the next two years. They predict the likelihood that you are going to default on a car payment, credit card payment, or other obligations. If you pay your bills on time, keep the balances low, and don't apply for too much credit, your score will be high no matter which version a potential creditor uses.

How your credit score changes

As I've mentioned, every time someone runs your credit, whether for a credit card or a personal loan, your credit score drops.

There are exceptions to this rule.

Question: All auto, student loan, mortgage-related inquiries made within 30 days of scoring are completely ignored.
True or False?

Answer: True

For example: if you apply for a car, mortgage, or student loan in a short period of time, usually within thirty days, these inquiries will be completely ignored. The scoring system can recognize when you are "rate shopping" or shopping for the best rate for a car, mortgage, or student loan. So, if you are car shopping and go to three different dealerships who all run your credit, your score will not drop because you are not looking for three car loans, just one. On the other hand, if you go to three different department stores and apply for a retail card at each of them, you are actually trying to get three cards, not one. In this case, your credit score will drop three times because you initiated credit at three stores, regardless of whether you were approved or denied.

If you don't pay your bills on time, your credit score drops. As mentioned earlier, if you file for bankruptcy, your credit score could plummet two or three hundred points. That's a huge drop and it takes years to recover.

While it is difficult to improve your FICO® score over the short term, you may improve your score over a period of time by:

1. Paying your bills on time.

2. Keeping the balances on your credit cards low, usually below 35% of the available credit.

3. Limiting the amount of new credit you apply for.

4. Making certain the information on your credit report is accurate and complete.

I checked my credit report and I have no credit yet at all.

For those of you who have no credit history at all, the very best way to establish a good credit score is to apply for a credit card. Certain companies are more lenient than others—Capital One, for example, tends to be easier than some other companies. If you cannot get one, then get a secured credit card. Once again, a secured credit card is a card where you give a deposit, usually two or three hundred dollars, to the bank. They put it in a savings account.

So, if the bank offers you a credit limit of $300 on your new secured credit card, then you will have to deposit $300 cash into your account as collateral. If you don't make the payments, the bank will cancel the card and deduct the amount owed to them from your deposit. After a year of making timely payments, the bank will return your deposit and you can become eligible for a regular, non-secured credit card. You just need to make sure that the bank reports to the credit bureaus. Most of them do, particularly the major banks. Bank of America, Capital One, and Wells Fargo all offer secured credit cards and report to the credit bureaus. A good place to start is at your local bank or credit union where you may already have a checking or savings account.

Credit cards can be a convenient way to track expenses, and are preferable to using a debit card in certain situations like online transactions, hotel or car reservations. Once you get a credit card, use it once, or use it only in need, but whatever your limit is, pretend like you have 35% of that limit and never go over that amount. So if your limit is $1,000, this card only has $350 as far as you're concerned. The reason you want to stay at 35% is that each creditor reports to the credit bureau at different times each month and they report what you owe at that moment. While you could actually max out and pay off your card each month, the credit card company might report before your payment comes in. For instance, Macy's may report the first of the month and Citibank may report on the fifteenth.

In addition, be conservative about applying for too many cards. Having too much available credit can spook creditors who may worry about the potential of you getting over your head in debt. There is no hard and fast rule indicating how many cards are too many, since it depends on the rest of your financial profile. Studies show that people generally spend more when they use plastic than when they use paper. That's because we tend to focus on the cost of a purchase when we have to hand over cash, versus just the benefits when we can simply swipe a card. And if you don't pay the balance off in full by the end of the monthly grace period, the interest may well eat up any rewards the card offers.

Ideally, I believe you should only have two or three cards. Hold on to one you use, cut the others up, and pay them on time each month out of direct deposit. That way you know it's paid on time every month, so you don't forget, because if you forget that one payment, then your credit score can really plummet.

Always keep in mind that the credit report you build is like a resume. While creditors do not want to see a history of mistakes, they don't want to see a blank page either. What they want to see is that you have experience managing credit wisely. This is especially true for someone looking to start building or rebuilding his credit, like someone who has just graduated from school or a friend or family member emerging from bankruptcy.

Lastly, make the monthly payments on time. You will see your score really go up.

Best credit cards for people who are new to the credit race:
1 Bank of America
2. Capital One
3. Chase
4. Citibank
5. Discover
6. Wells Fargo
7. Your local bank or credit union.

One last comment about credit

At the beginning of the chapter, I told you about my brother, his stellar credit history, and how that enabled him to buy a car at the best possible interest rate. What I neglected to mention is that we are African American. While this fact may or may not have had anything to do with the salesman's initial skepticism, I think it's important to mention that, contrary to some people's beliefs, credit ratings and scores DO NOT discriminate against people of color.

A credit score is nothing more than the output of a mathematical formula built to rank and order the likelihood that a person will repay the debts they have incurred.

The Federal Reserve Board (FRJ3) has studied the relationship between credit scores and race to see if empirically derived credit scores produce a disparate impact on specific populations. As part of that study, the FRB team compared credit scores from two types of models. One is a more traditional credit score and was developed on a national consumer population. The other type was a series of "race-neutral" models. Specifically, these models were developed for individual demographic populations (e.g., Hispanic, Black, Asian). Disparate impact would be apparent if a minority group scored higher on the race-neutral scorecard than on the baseline credit score. In other words, for each scoring model developed for a specific minority group, evidence of disparate impact would be found if this model yielded higher scores for the group than did the benchmark-scoring model.

On page 26 of their 2010 study, the FRB's Avery, Brevoort, and Canner wrote: "Our results provide little or no evidence that the credit characteristics used in credit history scoring models operate as proxies for race and ethnicity. The distributions of credit scores for different racial or ethnic groups or across genders are essentially unaffected by the re-estimation or redevelopment of the baseline credit scoring model in any of the race-or-gender-neutral environments. This suggests that credit scores do not have a disparate impact across race, ethnicity, or gender."

*Posted by Frederic Huynh on 09/11/2012 in Consumer Credit Risk, FICO® Score FAQ, Scoring Technology I Permalink

I mention this article because my own research on credit has proven to me that FICO® continues to build credit scores that are objective measures of risk, and has made great strides to demystify credit scores for consumers. They, like me, want to empower everyone, regardless of race, to become better managers of their credit.

With all of this information about FICO® and your credit score in mind, let's move on to the rules of the credit race!

CHAPTER THREE

The Rules of the Race
The Fair Credit Reporting Act

The Fair Credit Reporting Act was designed to help ensure that the information in your credit file is complete, accurate, and not outdated. The Federal Trade Commission (FTC) is the nation's consumer protection agency. It enforces the FCRA with respect to credit bureaus. The FCRA specifies who can access your credit report. Creditors, insurers, employers, and other businesses that use the information in your report to evaluate your applications for credit, insurance, employment, or renting a home have a legal right to access your report.

Your rights under the Fair Credit Reporting Act:

1. You have the right to receive a copy of your credit report. The copy of your report must contain all of the information in your file at the time of your request.

2. You have the right to know the name of anyone who received your credit report in the last year for most purposes, or in the last two years for employment purposes. Any company that denies your application must supply the name and address of the credit bureau they contacted, provided the denial was based on information given by the credit bureau.

3. You have the right to a free copy of your credit report when your application is denied because of information supplied by the credit bureau. Your request must be made within sixty days of receiving your denial notice.

4. If you contest the completeness or accuracy of information in your report, both the credit bureau and the furnisher of information are legally obligated to investigate your dispute.

How Do I Review My Credit Report?

Question: The only site where I can get a free report each year is <u>www.freecreditreport.com</u>.

True or False?

Answer: False

You can get credit reports elsewhere, but **<u>annualcreditreport. com</u>** is the only place that you can get a free credit report. At other sites, what you are getting is actually a monitoring service. They offer a free report, but it's only for a period of typically seven days. If you don't cancel after seven days, you pay a monthly charge to monitor your credit report.

Thanks to the **Fair Credit Reporting Act,** you are entitled to one free credit report from each of the three credit bureaus every 12 months. You won't be able to get free reports from the agencies directly, as they may charge up to $9.95 for each one. Only one website is authorized to fill orders for the free annual credit report you are entitled to under law, and that is **annualcreditreport.com.**

Other websites that claim to offer "free credit reports," "free credit scores," or "free credit monitoring" are not part of the legally mandated free annual credit report program. Some sites use terms like "free report" in their names; others have URLs that purposely misspell **annualcreditreport.com.** Be aware, some of these "imposter" sites may direct you to other sites that try to sell you something or collect your personal information.

Annualcreditreport.com and the three major credit bureaus will not send you an email asking for your personal information. If you get an email, see a pop-up ad, or get a phone call from someone claiming to be from **annualcreditreport.com** or any of the three nationwide credit bureaus , do not reply or click on any link in the message. It's probably a scam.

In fact, I suggest you forward any such email to the FTC at spam@ uce.gov.

You can request your free reports three ways:

1. Online: www.annualcreditreport.com

2. By Phone: 877-322-8228.

3. By Mail: Complete the Annual Credit Report Request Form and send it to the address below:

Annual Credit Report Request Service

P.O. Box 105281

Atlanta, GA

30348-5281

Reviewing your credit reports

Question: I should review my credit report at least twice a year. True or False?

Answer: False

Since there are three major credit bureaus, and you are entitled to three free reports a year, I strongly advise that you check each one, alternating the company, every four months. It's simple, and it's the very best way to protect you from inaccuracies and identity theft. Because nationwide credit bureaus get their information from different sources, the information in your report from one company may not reflect all, or exactly the same, information as the other two companies. That's not to say that the information in any of your reports is necessarily inaccurate, it just may be different, so be sure and check all three.

What information do I need to provide to get my free report?

You will need to provide your name, address, Social Security number, and date of birth. If you have moved in the last two years, you may have to provide your previous address. To maintain the security of your file, each credit bureau may ask you for some information that only you would know, like the amount of your monthly mortgage payment. Each company may ask you for different information because the information each has in your file may come from different sources.

Why do I want a copy of my credit report?

As I've mentioned, your credit report has information that affects whether you can get a loan and how much you will have to pay to borrow money. You also want to check your credit reports to make sure the information is accurate, complete, up-to-date, and to help guard against identity theft—which is when someone uses your personal information like your name, your Social Security number, or your credit card number to commit fraud. Identity thieves may use your information to open a new credit card account in your name. Then, when they don't pay the bills, the delinquent account is reported on your credit report. Inaccurate information like that can and may affect your ability to get credit, insurance, or even a job.

How long does it take to get my report after I order it?

If you request your report online at **annualcreditreport.com**, you should be able to access it immediately. If you order your report by calling toll-free 1-877-322-8228, your report will be processed and mailed to you within fifteen days. If you order your report by mail using the Annual Credit Report Request Form, your request will be processed and mailed to you within fifteen days of receipt.

Are there any situations where I might be eligible for additional free reports?

Under federal law, you're entitled to a free report if a company takes some course of adverse action against you, such as denying your application for credit, insurance, or employment, and you ask for your report within sixty days of receiving notice of the action. The notice will give you the name, address, and phone number of the credit bureau that provided that information. You're also entitled to one free report a year if you're unemployed and plan to look for a job within sixty days, if you're on welfare, or if your report is inaccurate because of fraud, including identity theft. Otherwise, a credit bureau may charge you up to $11 for another copy of your report within a 12-month period.

Question: According to a recent FCC study, 20% of all credit reports contain mistakes.
True or False?
> **Answer: True**
> Isn't this impetus enough to check your credit every four months?

About your file

Now that you are checking your credit report every four months, be aware that your credit file may not reflect all your credit accounts. Although most national department store and all-purpose bank credit card accounts will be included in your file, not all creditors supply information to the credit bureaus. Some retailers, credit unions, travel, entertainment, and gasoline card companies are among the creditors that don't.

When negative information in your report is accurate, only the passage of time can assure its removal. A credit bureau can report most accurate negative information for seven years, and bankruptcy information for ten years. There is a standard method for calculating the seven-year reporting period. Generally, the period runs from the date that the event took place. Information about an unpaid judgment against you can be reported for seven years or until the statute of limitations runs out, whichever is longer. There is no time limit on reporting information about criminal convictions, information reported in response to your application for a job that pays more than $75,000 a year, and information reported because you've applied for more than $150,000 worth of credit or life insurance.

What if I find errors?

According to Federal Trade Commission Consumer Education, if you inspect your credit report and find an error, you should report it to the credit bureau where the report originated. It's easiest to do this online via the website for each of the three agencies that issue credit reports. If your credit report is inaccurate, you can also write to each credit bureau. You'll want to include the following information:

1. Your full name

2. Mailing address

3. Credit report number (which is generally located in the top right corner of the report)

Tell the credit bureaus, in writing, what information you think is inaccurate. Tell the creditor or other information provider, in writing, that you dispute an item. Many providers specify an address for disputes. If the provider reports the item to a credit bureau, it must include a notice of your dispute. If the information is found to be inaccurate, the information provider may not report it again. Under the FCRA, both the credit bureau and the information provider (that is, the person, company, or organization that provides information about you to a credit bureau) are responsible for correcting inaccurate or incomplete information in your report.

Credit bureaus must investigate the items in question—usually within thirty days—unless they consider your dispute frivolous. They must forward all the relevant data you provide to the organization that provided the information. After the information provider receives notice of a dispute from the credit bureau, it must investigate, review the relevant information, and report the results back to the credit bureau. If the information provider finds the disputed information is inaccurate, it must notify all three nationwide credit bureaus so they can correct the information in your file.

When the investigation is complete, the credit bureau must give you the written results and a free copy of your credit report if the dispute results in a change. (This free report does not count as your annual free report.) If an item is changed or deleted, the credit bureau cannot put the disputed information back in your file unless the information provider later verifies that it is accurate and complete. The credit bureau also must send you written notice that includes the name, address, and phone number of the information provider.

If you tell the information provider that you dispute an item, a notice of your dispute must be included any time the information provider reports the item to a credit bureau.

Question: What can I do if the credit bureau or information provider won't correct the information I dispute?

Answer: If an investigation doesn't resolve your dispute with the credit bureau , you can ask that a statement of the dispute be included in your file, and in any and all future reports. You also can ask the credit bureau to provide your statement to anyone who received a copy of your report in the recent past. You may have to pay a fee for this service, however.

For more information:

The FTC works for the consumer to prevent fraudulent, deceptive, and unfair business practices in the marketplace and to provide information to help consumers spot, stop, and avoid them. To file a complaint, visit ftc.gov/complaint or call 1-877-FTC-HELP (1-877-382-4357). The FTC enters Internet, telemarketing, identity theft, and other fraud-related complaints into Consumer Sentinel, a secure online database available to hundreds of civil and criminal law enforcement agencies in the US and abroad.

Sample Dispute Letter

Date
Your Name
Your Address, City, State, Zip Code

Complaint Department
Name of Company
Address
City, State, Zip Code

Dear Sir or Madam:

I am writing to dispute the following information in my file. I have circled the items I dispute on the attached copy of the report I received.

This item (identify items disputed by name of source, and identify type of item, such as credit account, judgment, etc.) is (inaccurate or incomplete) because (describe what is inaccurate or incomplete and why). I am requesting that the item be removed (or request another specific change) to correct the information.

Enclosed are copies of (use this sentence if applicable and describe any enclosed documentation, such as payment records and court documents) supporting my position. Please re-investigate this (these) matter(s) and (delete or correct) the disputed item(s) as soon as possible.

Sincerely, Your name
Enclosures: (List what you are enclosing.)

CHAPTER FOUR

It's Performance that Counts
The Five Factors That Determine Your Credit Score

*J*anet came into my office eager to buy her first house. I was excited to help her—that was until I discovered she had a wallet overflowing with credit cards, all of which were maxed out, or close to it.

"Why do you have so many credit cards?" I asked her.

"Whenever the salesperson offers ten percent or more off, I go for it and save a bundle," she said.

"You also lose a bundle," I responded.

As she looked at me quizzically, I explained that because she didn't pay off the purchases she'd made in full before the bill came that first month, the interest she was paying monthly added up to a lot more than ten or fifteen percent off. Then, I gave her the really bad news. As a result of accumulating too much debt on too many credit cards, and more than a few late or missed payments, her FICO® score was so low that she couldn't qualify for the house she wanted to buy.

Even people who consider themselves bargain conscious can easily fall into the same trap as Janet, by applying for credit cards to get attractive incentives and then not paying them off immediately. In fact, the store credit cards are counting on most of us to do just that.

While it may be obvious that the discounts are quickly eaten up by interest payments, the effect of signing up for these cards, one after another, is much more insidious.

Getting and piling up debt on these seemingly minor credit accounts can be much more harmful to that all-important FICO® score than you ever thought, especially when you want to make a big, important purchase like a car or house.

You know by now I want everyone on my team to have a decent FICO® score—at least a 720 (or as close that perfect 850 as you can get)—to enable you to qualify for a major purchase and low interest rates on credit cards.

But how is it done?

There are five factors that determine your credit score:
1. Payment history
2. How much you owe
3. How long you've had credit
4. Your last application for credit
5. Types of credit you use

Let's look at each of these factors in depth:
1. Payment History
Question: My payment history affects my credit score more than any other factor.
True or False?
  Answer: True

Your payment history—that is whether you pay your bills on time, or as agreed, and how you've paid in the past, is the first and most important factor affecting your credit score. Thirty-five percent of your credit score is based on whether you've paid your bills on time and how you've paid in the past on any accounts that are reported to the credit bureau.

Have you paid your home, car, student loans, and credit cards on time or as agreed? What about your Home Depot card and your Gap bill? Seeing as this factor will determine over a third of your score, what do you think a third of your credit score will look like the month after a missed or late payment?

The main, and really only, exception here is medical bills. Medical bills are largely overlooked in the newest version of FICO® because you don't apply for credit when you are treated by a doctor and billed for his/her services. You may have gotten sick and most creditors don't believe the bills you receive as a result have anything to do with your credit worthiness. There just isn't the same statistical correlation. However, if you go out and get a car loan and don't pay it, or continually pay late, it does say something important about you and your habits.

So, don't be late!

Question: A 30-day late payment made today is not as bad as a 180-day late payment made six years ago.
True or False?

Answer: False

Keep in mind that most creditors, from MasterCard and Visa to the mortgage company, report every single month to each of the three credit bureaus. They report whether you pay, paid late, or don't pay at all. They report what your credit limit is, when your payment is due, when it was opened, and if you paid the account, late, how late: thirty, sixty, or more than ninety days late.

When it comes to negative information like late payments, the score focuses on these three factors:

How recent? If it is December and you were late in October, it is going to have a bigger negative effect than if you were late three years ago. The more recent the delinquency, the worse it affects your score.

How frequently are you late on your payments? One or two late payments are better than five or six late payments. How many months in a row were you thirty days late? Was it just once, or were there multiple months where you paid late? Obviously, both factors affect your score. If you are going to be late, you only want to be thirty days late once. Of course, you don't want to be late at all, but the less frequently, the better.

How severe? A payment that is thirty days late isn't as bad or serious as one that is sixty or ninety days late. Again, if you are going to be late, be late thirty days. Don't be late sixty days or ninety days. And, if you are late because of circumstances beyond your control, do your best to get current and stay current as soon as you can.

What constitutes a late payment?

I accidentally paid my Visa bill one week late. What do I do now?
Think of this as a false start and don't panic! You can be three, four, or even twenty-nine days late and the credit card company won't report you. What you can't be is thirty-one days late. They will only report you after thirty days. Mortgages, however, work a bit differently. If your mortgage payment is due the first day of the month, you are technically late on day two, but they give you a fifteen-day grace period. On the seventeenth day of the month, you will be assessed a late fee. But, as long as you get the payment in that month, it won't affect your credit score.

For you first-time homebuyers who are used to paying rent, I suggest you pretend the grace period doesn't exist. Mail the payment on the first. Better yet, set up some sort of electronic payment. As a housing and credit counselor, I hear too many stories about people legitimately mailing in their payment during the grace period, only to be assessed late charges because the payments sat on someone's desk for a week or so and weren't opened until the fifteenth or the sixteenth. I hate to think it, but I sometimes wonder if certain mortgage companies do this deliberately to collect late fees.

As a matter of course, be sure you pay all your bills on time. If you miss one payment of any kind, it affects your score. Do it the second month and you are going to see a huge drop in your credit score. Even a small payment of ten dollars that is ninety days late can hurt your credit rating more than a $2,000 payment that is thirty days late. It truly doesn't matter if it is $5 or $5,000,000. You are late. And, for those of you who typically pay on time and have good credit scores, keep in mind: the better the credit, the deeper the drop when a negative event occurs.

The moral of this story is simple: Pay the minimum if you need to, but pay on time and pay attention to those grace periods. One day past due and you are late. However, you are not reported late to the credit bureaus until you are more than thirty days late.

2. How much you owe

Also known as **Credit Utilization**, or **Balance to Credit Ratio**, how much you owe is the second most important factor affecting your credit score. This category, which accounts for 30% of your credit score, looks at and charts the total amount you owe on your accounts.

It is important to note that even if you pay your credit cards on time, if your **Credit Utilization** rate is too high, your credit score will drop. For example, let's say you have two credit cards with a total available credit of $2,000. If you use $500 on the first credit card and $700 on the second card, then you've used $1,200 of that $2,000. If you divide the 1,200 into the 2,000 you get a credit utilization ratio of 60%, which is almost double my recommended ratio of a maximum of 35%.

Credit Card #1 - $1,000.00 – Credit Limit
Credit Card #2 - $1,000.00 – Credit Limit
$2,000.00 – Total Credit

Charge $400.00 on Credit Card #1
Charge $200.00 on Credit Card #2
$600.00 - Total Charged on Cards

You have used $600.00 of your available credit of $2,000.00.

Balance to Credit Limit Ratio:
$600.00 / $2,000.00 = 30% (Low/Good)

Balance to Credit Limit Ratio

As you can see, if you pay down your balances, your credit score increases. If you keep your credit cards as low as possible, your credit score will remain stable. Always try to pay down the balances on your credit cards. People with really good credit typically only use about 7% of their available credit. So, if you want to be really in the top you want to keep it at zero or as close to zero as possible, but 35% is absolute maximum.

Question: When I get my credit card balances to zero, I should close the account.
True or False?
Answer: False

Never close an account once you've opened it, particularly if you've paid it off; the account has a positive status, and the balance is zero. Why? It will reduce your **Credit Utilization** ratio. So, for instance if you have a total of $10,000 in available credit and you owe $5000, your credit utilization rate is 50%. Assume that you pay off, in full, one of your department store cards that had a credit line of $4,000. Now your utilization rate here is a healthy 35%. If, however, you close the paid-off department credit card, your credit utilization shoots back up to 50%. Remember, as a general rule, it is best to keep your credit card balances as low as possible. The maximum should not exceed 35% of your available credit.

How many credit cards do I need?

If you have two or three credit cards, you have all you ever need. You really don't need anybody else running your credit. You don't need those department store credit cards at all. Assuming you already have them though, don't cancel them. As I've said, the more cards you have (assuming they are paid down) the better your credit utilization rate.

What should you do with them, then?

Cut them up.

Make sure you have a record of what they are, and the account number associated with them, and cut them up. It's the only way to make sure you won't use them unnecessarily.

3. How long you've had credit

Also known as the **Length of Credit History**, this factor accounts for 15% of your credit score. While much less important than the previous two factors, the longer you've had credit, the better.

This score considers both of the following:

A. The average age of your oldest accounts.

B. The average age of all your accounts.

It stands to reason that a person with a long stable history of credit is going to have a higher score than someone who is just starting out. Use the credit you have wisely and this score will continue to increase over time.

4. Your last application for credit:

How much new credit have you taken out? For how much? Your most recent applications for credit account for 10% of your score. This category is also known as **How Much New Credit,** and looks at how much new debt you are taking on in an attempt to determine if you could potentially become overextended.

Is it starting to make sense now that if you go to the mall this weekend and apply for credit cards in eight different stores, in order to save 10 or 15% or whatever incentive each of the stores is offering, your credit score could take an immediate nosedive of 50 to 60 points?

> **This score factors in the following:**
> **A. The number of accounts you've recently applied for.**
> **B. The number of new accounts you've opened.**
> **C. How much time has passed since you applied for credit.**
> **D. How much time since you've opened an account.**

What if I'm shopping for a car, and go to two or three dealerships and inquire about credit terms to get my best deal?

This is an exception for exactly that reason. As mentioned in an earlier chapter, your FICO® score completely ignores auto, mortgage, and student loan inquiries made in the last thirty days. Then, after the thirty-day period, all auto etc., inquiries made within 45 days of each other are combined into one.

While shopping for the best car or mortgage loan makes solid financial sense, opening multiple credit card accounts in a short time does not. A motto to live by (for a variety of reasons) is be really careful about who you are giving your Social Security number to. When I see my clients are first-time homebuyers, I give them all the same warning:

"Listen to me carefully. At this point no one gets your Social Security number until you own this house. If someone wants your Social Security number, you call me. That means you give it to no one."

Why?

I've seen it happen where prospective homeowners got so excited they went out and financed furniture for their new home before the house closed. As a result, their credit score dropped, and they didn't get the house because they suddenly had too much debt.

If I had a megaphone, this is the training moment when I'd shout: "ONLY OPEN UP ACCOUNTS YOU NEED AND DON'T CHARGE THEM UP TO THE LIMIT!"

5. Types of credit you use

Also known as your **Credit Mix**, this category accounts for 10% of your overall score. It tends to be much more important if you do not have other information on which to base a credit score. In other words, it is better to have both installment debt (a car loan, for example) and revolving debt (credit card) than just having all installment debt. They want to see a mix of how you pay different kinds of debt. One caveat, here: if you don't currently have installment debt, don't go out and get it just for the sake of your credit score!

Elements of your FICO® Score

30%
How much
you owe

10%
Types of credit
you use

HOW A
FICO®
SCORE
BREAKS
DOWN

15%
How long
you've had
credit

35%
Payment History

10%
Your last
application
for credit

What does my FICO® score really mean?

A FICO® score does one thing: It determines the likelihood that you will become ninety days or more delinquent on a credit obligation within the next two years. In other words, it predicts the likelihood that you are going to default within a given time period.

"FICO® scores have a significant impact on consumers' ability to get loans and other credit, and on the interest rate they receive. They are used in 90% of consumer-lending decisions," according to CEB TowerGroup, a financial services research firm.

Knowing your FICO® scores can give you an indication of whether you are likely to get approved for a new loan. If you have a low score, you can delay applying and work on improving it.

Also, a sudden dive in the score can be a warning that someone has fraudulently opened accounts in your name.

If your score is:

300-550: Credit is going to be hard to come by. Very.

550-600: You might be able to get a loan but it is going to be at an exorbitant rate.

600-680: You are considered a decent credit risk, but you may have some troubles here or there. It means you've had some late payments.

680-720: Means you will have decent credit and should not have trouble getting approved for most loans or credit cards.

720-780: You are in the second tier of those with great credit. No problems getting approved for loans or credit cards with low rates.

Above 780: You have stellar credit and they are going to give you tons of credit.

Average scores:

About 35% of us consumers now have FICO® scores under 650. The average score in America is 695, which is an all-time high. However, the average credit score varies among age groups and income levels. For example, FICO scores tend to improve with age and the higher one's income, the higher their credit scores tends to be. Also, about 14% of the U.S. population has no credit score, and are called credit invisible.

Interest rates based on scores:

Varying scores will affect the interest rates a consumer is charged. For example, if borrowers with a 720 or higher FICO® score got an average 3.183% annual percentage rate on a 36-month car loan for a new vehicle, borrowers with a score between 690 and 719 were offered an average APR of 4.546% according to Infonna Research Services, a market research firm.

Beating the odds

Since you are reading this book, you are playing on my team, and my team is not playing to be average, but to win. Play for the win by paying your bills on time, keeping your balances as low as possible, and not applying for any new, unnecessary credit cards or other debt.

Chapter Five

False Starts

Myths about Credit

Question: If a ninety-year-old woman wants to buy a house with a thirty-year mortgage, can she get a loan if her credit is good?

Answer: Yes

Surprised? Many people are.

While it is extremely unlikely that a ninety-year-old will live long enough to pay off such a mortgage, it is also true that a thirty-year-old could be hit by a truck leaving the closing for his home. Because of this, mortgage lenders must base their decisions solely on your credit, not your age, unless the consumer is applying for a reverse mortgage where the borrower must be at least 62 years or older to qualify. In fact, age-dependent credit is a sheer myth. Mortgage companies can't discriminate based on age. The Equal Employment Opportunity Commission (EEOC) won't allow it.

There are a number of other common myths about credit.

Let's take a look:

Closing accounts will help your score.

As I mentioned in the previous chapter, this is a commonly held misconception. It is also a bad mistake.

Why?

Assume you have two credit cards.

Credit Card #1 has a limit of $1,000.

Credit Card #2 also has a limit of $1,000.

You have $2,000 of total available credit on both cards.

Now, assume you charge $300 on Credit Card #1 and $800 on Credit Card #2 for a total of $1,100.

You have used $1,100 of your total available credit of $2,000.

Your Balance to Credit Limit Ratio is $1,100 /$2,000 = 55%

If you pay off and close Credit Card #1, the Balance to Credit Ratio is 80% (High). If you do the same to Credit Card #2, the Balance to Credit Ratio is 30% (Low). A high Balance to Credit Ratio (or Utilization Rate) will hurt your Credit Score.

As a rule, it is best to keep the Balance to Credit Ratio (or Utilization Rate) below 35%, so pay off your cards and cut them up, but keep the accounts open.

Why Not to Close Credit Cards with Zero Balances

Credit Card #1 - $1,000.00 – Credit Limit
Credit Card #2 - $1,000.00 – Credit Limit
                 $2,000.00 – Total Credit

Charge $300.00 on Credit Card #1
Charge $800.00 on Credit Card #2
       $1,100.00 - Total Charged on Cards

You have used $1,100.00 of your available credit of $2,000.00.

Balance to Credit Limit Ratio:
$1,100.00 / $2,000.00 = 55% (High/Bad)

If you close Credit Card #1, and leave open Credit Card #2, the Balance to Credit Ratio is now 80%
$800.00 / $1,000.00 = 80% (Very High/Bad)

You can hurt your score by checking your own credit.

This is also untrue. As I've also mentioned, there are three major credit bureaus in the United States. Thanks to federal law, you are entitled to one free credit report from each of them, every 12 months. Just as a reminder, the only truly free site on which to order yours is: **www.annualcreditreport.com.** All others are imposters.

You can hurt your score by shopping for the best rate.

Shopping for the best car or mortgage loan makes solid financial sense. However, opening multiple credit card accounts in a short period of time does not. Because of this, your FICO® score completely ignores auto, mortgage, and student loan inquiries made in a thirty-day period. Then, after the thirty-day period, all auto, mortgage or student loan inquiries made within forty-five days of each other are combined into one.

Your credit merges with your new spouse's when you marry.

This is a very important fallacy. Two do not become one where credit scores are concerned.

As a broker, there is nothing worse than telling a bright-eyed young couple looking to buy their first home, "Sorry, but your husband (or wife) can't be on the loan."

Going on to explain that we can't use his or her income to factor in the house they would otherwise qualify for is even worse.

This scenario happens all too often amongst the couples I work with, because either the wife or the husband has bad credit an overwhelming majority of the time. Rarely do I get a husband and wife on the mortgage together. When this situation occurs, my clients are forced to settle for a house in a neighborhood well below their combined means, all because one of them has a low credit score and the mortgage company or bank can't use his or her income to qualify them for a loan.

While a lot of people, especially younger people, have credit problems, somehow this seems to be one of those taboo relationship subjects. I find it interesting that two people can fall in love, be romantic with each other, decide to get married, and never discuss the fact that one of them has six judgments or a tax lien. In fact, one might argue that perhaps he or she has been a bit dishonest in the relationship. I am not saying your spouse-to-be is not the love of your life, but if you're willing to spend the rest of your life with someone, don't you think you need to know more about him than his favorite color?

When I say this in my seminars, people don't always know how to take it, at least at first. Then I explain that if you are about to marry somebody and they have bad credit, it will absolutely affect you. If the husband's credit is bad and you can't use his income, it affects how much house you can buy. And what about the wedding costs? Are you going to try and get credit cards together to pay for things? What about a car loan? You are potentially setting yourself up for failure on some levels. I am not saying you don't marry this person, but if they are not being responsible with their personal finances, maybe you should look at how they spend money and pay their bills before you walk down the aisle.

At some point, someone will always speak up at my seminar and say, "I wish I had known my husband (or wife) had bad credit."

There's always someone else in the crowd who is willing to volunteer the information, "My husband (or wife), I thought he made good money and I thought he had good credit, until we tried to buy a house or a car."

I hate questioning people who are in love, but I've seen the credit score inequity scenario so many times, I believe that bringing up this topic before there can be any disappointment or strife promotes an openness that allows people to work stronger, towards better credit and an even more solid relationship.

Too many inquiries will not hurt your credit score.

We are far enough into the book that you should know the answer to this one is FALSE. Your most recent applications for credit account for 10% of your FICO® score. This category of the score, which is also known as **How Much New Credit,** looks at how much new debt you are taking on in an attempt to determine if you could potentially become overextended.

In short, DO NOT go to the mall and apply for credit cards at every store that offers you an incentive to do so. Your credit score will take an immediate nosedive.

It's good to have some debt.

This is a fallacy. Use a credit card to establish some credit, but then pay it off as soon as possible. First of all, the longer it takes to pay it off, the more interest you pay. More important, 30% of your credit score is comprised of how much of your available credit you actually use. The more you use and the closer you get to your credit limit, the more your score drops.

The people with the highest credit scores only use 7%, on average, of their available credit. While that doesn't work for everyone, the lower the better. I recommend that you never exceed 35% of your available credit limit.

Co-signing for a friend or family member will not affect your credit report.

Co-signing is a huge no-no. It is also a huge topic for me that we'll talk about in more depth a little later in the book. For the moment, I'll just say that I've never seen anything good come out of co-signing. What I have seen is people who have suffered a heavy price because they co-signed or got a mortgage for one of their children who couldn't qualify due to bad credit. In turn, the children, who had already proven themselves less than responsible, didn't pay the mortgage and the house was foreclosed on them. When the children walk away from the house, the parent who was trying to "help out" is left with the ruined credit. After all, the bank doesn't care that your daughter promised she would pay the bill on time and then lost her job or blew her money on a cruise. The bank also doesn't care that she's learned her lesson and is really going to change *next time*. All they know is they didn't get paid as promised, and you are on the line for someone else's reckless behavior.

A short sale is better than a foreclosure on your credit report.

A short sale is the sale of a property in which the proceeds from the sale will not be enough to pay off the existing mortgage. In this case, the lender may allow the borrower to sell the property, accept an amount that is less than what is owed on the mortgage, and release the borrower from the loan. While it's true that a lot of banks are accepting short sales and real estate agents commonly tell homebuyers that a short sale is better than a foreclosure, a short sale and a foreclosure affect your credit score the same. The reason? FICO® determined that one out of every two borrowers who had a short sale went on to default on another account within the next two years. In other words, borrowers who have a short sale on their records have the same bad habits as people who foreclose on their loans. So, whether you have a short sale or foreclosure, your score is going to be affected. The worse news is the higher your score before the short sale, the bigger the drop.

How Mortgage Delinquencies (and other events) Affect FICO® Score

	Consumer A	Consumer B	Consumer C
Starting FICO® Score	680	720	780
FICO® Score after these events:			
30 days late on mortgage	600-620	630-650	670-690
90 days late on mortgage	600-620	610-630	650-670
Short sale / deed-in-lieu settlement (no deficiency balance)	610-630	605-625	655-675
Short sale (with deficiency balance)	575-595	570-590	620-640
Foreclosure	575-595	570-590	620-640
Bankruptcy	530-550	525-545	540-560

This chart breaks down how many points you would lose if you are thirty, sixty, or ninety days late on a foreclosure or bankruptcy. As you can see, the higher the credit score, the more points you will lose. The reason? If you have good credit, it means you have historically paid your bills on time. If you have a 620 you have been late more than once. That's how you got a 620 in the first place. The scoring system kind of expects you to be late a few times. At an 800 credit score, the scoring system is not expecting you to be late, so when you are late it is kind of like a warning bell. If it is a one-time event, your credit will rebound quicker than someone with a lower score, but if you are late a second month, it is assumed there is something signifi-cant going on and your score will crash.

The lesson in this chart?

Once you have good credit, you have to continue to pay your bills on time. In athletic terms, once you're on top, there's nowhere to go but down.

Only a credit repair company can repair your credit.

This is such an important topic that I will be devoting an entire up-coming chapter to it. For now, know that this is not only false, but there is very little a credit repair company can do that you can't do yourself. Worse, they charge you a fee, sometimes an exorbitant one, to do something you can and should do for free. The bottom line is you are way better off avoiding credit repair companies altogether. How? Hang tight—I will show you how to repair your credit and change your behavior so you don't get back into trouble ever again, a few chapters from now.

Employers can check your credit without your permission.

An employer cannot run a credit check on you without your permis-sion. No one can ever run your credit without your permission. Be advised however, that an application may have the permission em-bedded somewhere that states that they can run your credit. When you apply for a job, you need to ask an employer, "Are you running my credit?" Otherwise, they may not even mention to you that they are checking.

I had a friend who went to a job interview and was told he was a good candidate, only to be denied because of his credit. This gentle-man happened to be a real estate broker; he had very good credit, but had lost a lot of his business during the real estate crash. When he couldn't pay credit cards on time, he did what he could, and started getting behind. He was applying for a job so he could start paying his bills, but wasn't hired because of his recent credit issues.

Unfair, right?

The EEOC has repeatedly acknowledged that the use of credit checks to screen out job applicants disproportionately impacts wom-en and minorities, and therefore could be evidence of workplace bias.

THE RACE FOR GOOD CREDIT • 61

California, Colorado, Connecticut, Delaware, Hawaii, Illinois, Maryland, Nevada, Oregon, Vermont and Washington have enacted legislation limiting or banning companies from running credit checks. While the EEOC wants to amend the Fair Credit Reporting Act to ban this practice, and these 11 states and some cities like New York City have done so, nothing has changed on the national level just yet. There was a federal effort by U.S. Representative Steve Cohen and U.S. Senator Elizabeth Warren, who sought sponsors for their legislation known as "The Equal Employment for All Act." This act would have prohibited employers from using credit checks as part of their hiring and promotion practices except in some circumstances, i.e., a position that requires national security clearance. This act did not pass, however, and new legislation should be introduced.

Race and gender are factored into your credit score.

When I ask people whether they believe race and gender are factored into credit scores, the answer seems to depend on what race of folks I'm talking to. Whites generally say it's false. Blacks tend to say it's true. Some people even think where you live and your income are factored into the score.

Your credit score does not take into consideration race, gender, marital status, religion, national origin, income, or where you live. And while some people may suspect otherwise, there is plenty of research showing that blacks who have similar credit profiles as whites have the same scores. If you pay your bills the same as another person, and you have similar profiles, your scores are going to look the same. On a personal note, over the years I've looked at literally thousands of credit reports and I truly believe it is a pretty objective and unbiased factor.

Discrimination, such that it is, is not coming from the scores. The sad truth is that it is coming from the people actually reviewing the scores and loaning the money. For example, research supports the fact that women who walk into a car dealership alone historically pay a higher interest rate than men. There are studies involving Latinos and African Americans proving that even when they had good credit, they were put into subprime loans. (These are loans for people with less than stellar credit.) A lot of African Americans and Latinos who had 800 credit scores got an interest rate of, say, 8% when they should have been getting 3-4%. This is a clear example of why knowledge is power.

Why? For one thing, they were discriminated against because they didn't know they had good scores. They didn't know what a good score was. They weren't asking the question, *what is my credit score?* When they were told they would be approved for a loan, but at an interest rate of 8%, they agreed without knowing they qualified for an interest rate of about 4%.

I would say most people are probably getting higher rates than their credit score dictates. The government has done a lot to correct this problem, but they can only do so much. While things have certainly equalized a great deal over the years, there is an easy solution to feeling discriminated against on any basis—know your scores, read all paperwork, and go into transactions empowered and understanding the significance of your credit score.

CHAPTER SIX

Disqualifiers
Identity Theft

Identity Theft is defined as the misuse of your personal identifying information, such as your name and Social Security number, credit card numbers, or other financial account information, to commit fraud and other crimes. The Federal Trade Commission (the FTC) estimates that ten to twelve million Americans have their identities stolen each year. Since there's a new identity theft in the US every four seconds, you or someone you know has experienced some form of identity theft.

This crime can take many forms. Identity thieves may rent an apartment, obtain a credit card, or establish a telephone account in your name. You may not find out about the theft until you review your credit report or a credit card statement and notice charges you didn't make, or until you're contacted by a debt collector.

While some identity theft victims may resolve their problems quickly, others spend hundreds of dollars and untold hours repairing damage to their good name and credit record. The Identity Theft Resource Center says that many victims spend 300-600 hours to recover their good name and recover financially. According to the FTC, about 5% of all identity theft involves victims under the age of 18. Some consumers victimized by identity theft may lose job opportunities, or be denied loans for education, housing or cars because of negative information on their credit reports. In rare cases, they may even be arrested for crimes they did not commit.

How Do Identity Thieves Steal Your Identity?

1. Dumpster Diving – Thieves actually go through your trash looking for bills or other papers with personal information on them.

2. Phishing – Thieves pretend to be financial institutions or companies and send spam or pop-up messages to get you to reveal your personal information. They will then call the financial companies and pretend that they are you and get information. As in, "Hi, I am Trent. I lost my wallet" or "I lost my information but I can give you…" Since they already know some information, and they may have your Social Security number, they may order another credit or debit card in your name.

3. Changing your address – Thieves divert your billing statements to another location by completing a change of address form. They have your credit card number and say they've moved and to send the statements to their new address. They start using the credit card and you don't get a bill. By the time you realize the bill isn't coming and contact the company, they have charged up your credit card.

4. Old-fashioned Stealing – Thieves steal wallets, purses, mail—including bank and credit statements, pre-approved credit offers, and new checks or tax information. They also steal personnel records from businesses and/or bribe employees who have access.

5. Pretext – Thieves use false pretenses to get personal information from financial institutions, e.g., credit card offers.

What do thieves do with a stolen identity?

1. Credit Card Fraud

Thieves open credit cards in your name and do not pay the bill. When they use the cards and don't pay the bills, the delinquent accounts appear on your credit report.

2. Phone or Utilities Fraud

Thieves open a new phone or wireless account in your name or run up charges on your existing account. They may change the billing address on your credit card so that you no longer receive bills, and then run up charges on your account. Because your bills are now sent to a different address, it may be some time before you realize there's a problem. They may also use your name to get utility service like electricity, heating, or cable TV.

3. Bank/Finance Fraud

Thieves may create counterfeit checks using your name or account number. They may open a bank account in your name and write bad checks. They may clone your ATM or debit card and make electronic withdrawals in your name, draining your accounts. They may even take out a loan in your name.

4. Government Documents Fraud

Thieves may get a driver's license or official ID card issued in your name but with their picture. They may use your name and Social Security number to get government benefits. They may even file a fraudulent tax return using your information.

5. Other Fraud

Thieves may rent a house or get medical services using your name. They may get a job using your Social Security number. Scariest of all, they may give your personal information to police during an arrest. When they don't show up for court, a warrant may be issued for your arrest.

The Most Surprising Identity Theft of All

When I was a housing counselor, young people in their early twenties would come in with one or two delinquencies on their credit report from when they were under ten years old. I quickly learned that parents with bad credit used their children's personal information—often when the gas or some other utility was turned off and they wanted to put a different name on the account to restore service. Seeing as they have their child's personal information, they used his or her name and the gas bill soon came to the house addressed to their four-year-old.

I also saw this happen between grown siblings. If you live with your sister, for example, you can just go up to her bedroom and get her Social Security number. You know her birthday, and you know where she lives, so it is easy for you to go and apply for a credit card in her name.

Even when identity theft isn't in the family, thieves prey upon the identities of the very young and older people. After all, no one is checking the credit of minors. And a lot of older people aren't making large or frequent purchases so their credit is stable, making them perfect targets.

Unfortunately, many people learn that their identity has been stolen when the bill collection agency contacts them for an overdue debt they never incurred, they apply for a mortgage or car loan and the loan is held up due to something on their credit report , or they receive some correspondence about an apartment they never rented or a job they never held.

The best way to stay on top of this is to monitor your accounts and bank statements each month, and check your credit report on a regular basis. If you check your credit report regularly, you may be able to limit the damage caused by identity theft. If you are doing it three to four times a year, it's much easier to catch an irregularity right away and get it corrected.

What should you do if your identity is stolen?

Don't delay in correcting your records and contacting all companies that opened fraudulent accounts. Make the initial contact by phone, then follow up in writing. The longer the fraudulent information goes uncorrected, the longer it will take to resolve the problem.

Should you file a police report if your identity is stolen?

While you may not need to contact police if the thief made charges on an existing account and you have been able to work with the company to resolve the dispute, filing a police report, checking your credit reports, notifying creditors, and disputing any unauthorized transactions are some of the steps you may need to take. A police report that provides specific details of the identity theft is called an Identity Theft Report. It entitles you to certain legal rights when provided to the credit bureaus or to companies where the thief misused your information. An Identity Theft Report can be used to permanently block fraudulent information from appearing on your credit report. It will also make sure these debts do not reappear on your credit reports. Identity Theft Reports can prevent a company from continuing to collect debts from identity theft, or selling them to others for collection. An identity theft report is also needed to place an extended fraud alert on your credit report.

You should also file an ID Theft Complaint with the FTC and bring your printed ID Theft Complaint with you to the police station when you file your police report. This complaint can be used to support your local police report to ensure that it includes the detail required.

How Long Do the Effects of Identity Theft Last?

It's difficult to predict how long the effects of identity theft will linger. That's because it depends on many factors, including the type of theft, whether the thief sold or passed your information on to other thieves, whether the thief is caught, and problems related to correcting your credit report.

If you are the victim of identity theft, you should monitor financial records for several months after you discover the crime. If you review your credit reports once every four months as I've recommended, you will be on top of anything suspicious from here on out. From then on, stay alert for other signs of identity theft.

Fighting Identity Theft

Jim was on vacation. Upon check-in at his hotel in South Beach, the woman at the registration desk asked to copy his driver's license, credit card, and the back of the credit card with the security code. He thought it was odd, but soon forgot about it. He arrived in the Bahamas a few days later, only to find out that five thousand dollars' worth of items had been charged on his card and three accounts had been opened in three days. Fortunately, he'd called the credit card company before he left town to tell them where he'd be and they contacted him because of the suspicious activity. The card company reversed the charges.

If you are going to travel, you take one card and you let the credit card company know you are going to be away, where, and when. If somebody in your city, or anywhere other than where you've said you are going to be, uses the card during that period, they know there's something wrong.

These days, with computer technology and all the information floating around on the Internet, hackers think nothing of sending your contacts emails fraudulently pretending to be you and asking them, *"Help me, I'm stranded at the airport in the Philippines and need money."*

It's not only hard, it's sometimes seemingly impossible to protect ourselves from identity theft. While you can certainly sign up for one of those credit monitoring services that will alert you within twenty-four hours about any suspicious activity and any changes to your credit report, and definitely should if your identity has already been stolen, I still maintain that some very old-fashioned precautions are key to ensuring the safety of your identity:

1. Shred everything.

Don't just rip it up, but shred anything with your name, address, or account numbers—particularly bank statements. You must use a cross-shredder. A lot of times people take credit card statements, old ones, and put them in the garbage. Thieves may not get your full credit card information but they still have your personal information. Thieves definitely go through dumpsters, especially behind businesses. We have had our trash stolen at my real estate office because thieves assume we toss out paperwork containing Social Security numbers, bank statements, driver's licenses, pictures, and the like. Fortunately, we have a strict policy of destroying everything. Nothing goes into the trash with any personal information.

2. Protect all of your ID.

You can't leave important paperwork or documents just lying around in an office. Do you have roommates? If so, don't leave your checkbook, ID, and credit cards out and accessible. Once again, shred any statements that someone else could get a hold of.

3. Be wary about handing off your credit card and ID to anyone who asks.

Especially if they leave your sight with your personal information. Armed with the knowledge of how to protect yourself and take action, you can make identity thieves' jobs much more difficult. You can also help fight identity theft by educating your friends, family, and members of your community about how to protect themselves as well.

CHAPTER SEVEN

Credit Fit at Any Age
Credit Through the Years

Adivorced friend of mine has a daughter. The woman's father died and left his home to her when she was 23.

She lost the house i

n three years.

How did she lose a house that was given to her free and clear in such a short time? Actually, it was fairly easy. She didn't pay her real estate taxes and lost the house in a tax sale, because she was more interested in spending her money on Michael Kors purses and going on cruises than paying taxes on her one and only important asset. Had she been responsible enough to actually be a homeowner, and sold the house from the outset, she probably could have cleared a profit of about $80k.

Instead, she ended up with nothing.

When I got wind of the situation, I asked, "They must owe you the difference between the tax payment and what the house was worth, right?"

Her answer?

"I heard someone talking about that, but I didn't want to deal with them."

Ten years have passed, and she's not only still doing the same irresponsible things, she's usually asking someone to lend her money. As you might imagine, her credit more than reflects her questionable financial choices.

So do her opportunities.

While this is an extreme example of irresponsible behavior, we all know it's a lot more fun and easy to get caught up in what we want to buy, not what we need to do to protect our assets and credit. Although young people are more likely to make these kinds of mistakes, simply because they don't understand how it all works, everyone faces financial and credit issues at different stages throughout their lives. Really, it doesn't matter what age you are. People getting out of school tend to get caught up with all the things they can buy simply by pulling out a piece of plastic. The married-with-kids crowd can easily get overextended by the combination of the "big" purchases and too many credit cards. Then it's trying to save for retirement while putting the kids through college. For the retired crowd, there's the threat of losing whatever savings and equity you've accumulated.

While a seventy-nine-year-old can find himself dealing with an issue commonly faced by a person a third of his age, there are credit issues endemic to certain age groups. In this chapter, we will look at these issues and the best solutions to overcome them.

Millennials (Ages 18-34)

One day, a client pulled up to my office in a beautiful black Lexus. He came in, sat down, and announced that he was 23, owned a duplex, and needed assistance because he was three months behind on his mortgage payments.

I questioned him about his mortgage. As it turned out, he lived in one unit, and had a tenant living in the other who paid $525. His mortgage was $550 so, technically, he was paying $25 in rent.

Why then, was he behind?

Along with his rent, he had a car note for $800 and auto insurance of $300 for an additional total of $1,100 month.

"Since you're three months behind on your mortgage, I assume you must be three months behind on your car note," I said.

"Oh, no," he said, just as I expected. "I'm current on my car note because my mother helps me pay that."

"Okay," I said. "Since your tenant pays all but $25 of your mortgage, why not add $25 to that payment and pay the mortgage, then?"

The thought completely befuddled him.

So did my next bit of advice: "Take that car back."

He looked at me as though I'd lost my mind as I continued on. "You live in the city of Philadelphia. We have a great mass transit system. You have buses that run all over but you are paying $1,100 a month just to drive a five-year-old Lexus. For that kind of money, I would expect you to drive up in a Bentley. Return that car and you eliminate $1,100 from your monthly expenses."

Needless to say, he ignored my advice.

Six months later, however, he did come back—this time on the bus. He thanked me and admitted that he got rid of the car after he lost his property. Following my advice would have saved him from ruining his credit and losing his house.

Millennials are, by definition, the most affected by having good credit.

Why? Millennials have shorter credit histories than any other age group. Unfortunately, because of their naiveté about credit, they have more delinquent payments as well. As a result, approximately 28% of Millennials have scores in the 300-579 range, compared to only 19% of the total population.

Millennials, who make up a full 25% of the population, are looking to open new credit more than any other group. They also have the largest number of credit inquiries, because of their age and their new entry into the workforce. They're young and they're usually applying for credit for the first time. They're in college, or coming out of college, so are very likely to be seeking a car note and, not too long after, their first mortgage.

Unfortunately, and as the above story demonstrates, getting, understanding, and maintaining good credit can be a tricky prospect.

Best Advice for Millennials:

1. In order to generate a credit score, you need at least one account that's been open, and hasn't been in dispute, for six months.

The best way to do this is to apply for a credit card. If you can't get one, open a secured credit card with your local bank or credit union. Just be certain you aren't applying for a card that's going to charge you a really high interest rate or APR (the difference between the actual interest rate and all the fees). Be sure and compare rates by looking at what the interest rate will be, what the terms are, if they charge you a monthly processing fee, and what they charge as an annual fee. You should also look into the history of the credit card company. Despite the offers that show up in the mail, the cards with the best rates are often the most recognizable in terms of names.

Best credit cards for people new to the credit race:
Bank of America
Capital One
Chase
Citibank
Discover
Wells Fargo
Your local bank or credit union.

2. Don't overextend yourself.

What I mean here is DO NOT get more credit cards than you need. I recommend a maximum of three cards, two of which you don't use. Credit cards are more predictive of default, so keep them paid, on time, and it will raise your score faster than any other type of credit.

3. Do not allow yourself to develop bad habits.

Make sure you pay at least the minimum on your credit cards and other obligations on time. In other words, handle the credit you have responsibly. If you do, it will not only allow you to get that car or mortgage loan, but also at the best possible terms.

4. Create a budget.

Budgets keep us in line. We know what we're spending. I always tell people there should be a name on every dollar. In other words, every dollar should be earmarked for some expense, i.e. rent, the car note, the student loan, and, yes, even entertainment. (But not $10,000 in entertainment unless you have enough income to support such an expense.) Once you can say where every dollar goes, you have yourself a good working budget and know what you have left over for extras.

Important Additional Information for Millennials

Student Loans:
Question: Carrying high student loan debt will hurt my credit score. True or False?
Answer: False

Student loan debt is treated like any installment debt. Just as if you had a mortgage for $200,000, pay it on time, and you won't have any issues whatsoever where your credit is concerned. Student loan debt can factor into FICO® scores, but credit card debt has a larger impact since credit card indebtedness has a stronger statistical correlation with future borrower performance than does installment debt. In other words, paying your credit cards (or resolving debt) on time will increase your credit score faster than any other form of credit.

Car Loans:

While my best advice is don't buy the car without cash, we all want and sometimes need those shiny wheels. If you have to take the plunge, buy a slightly used car, because you lose money on the depreciation the second you drive off the lot in a new car.

Not convinced, or more likely, still convinced you have to have that bright, shiny, new car? Assuming you have a down payment, and don't need someone to co-sign for you, buy the car in the best way possible—meaning don't take the offer from the car dealership's finance company right off the bat. Instead, go to your bank or your credit union. Chances are, their terms are much better than at the car dealership. Believe it or not, the bank or credit union interest rate could be 12% to 15% cheaper.

If your bank and credit union won't give you a loan on the car, maybe that's telling you something you should be listening to. If they reject you or offer you less than prime rates, take whatever money you were going to put down and buy something that gets you from here to there until your credit is established enough that you can get the terms you want.

Otherwise, you'll be paying far too much.

According to information from Informa Research Services, a market research company, if your credit score is between 720 and 850 and you purchase a new car for $30,000.00 (and the APR is 3.45%), your monthly payment is $878.00. Over a 36-month term, you will pay back $1,625.00 in interest to the finance company. Conversely, if you have a credit score between 500 and 589, the APR will be much higher – around 15.09% - and your monthly payment is $1,041.00. Over that same 3-year period, you will pay $7,491.00 in interest. In other words, you will pay a total of $37,491.00 for your new car (compared to $31,635.00 if you had a better credit rating). The lesson here: bad credit is very expensive.

Employment

According to The Society of Human Resource Management, the number of employers who conducted pre-employment credit checks is on the rise, up from 36% to 43%.

This is not surprising since I hear people say a lot, "Well, this job ran my credit..."

When an employer asks for a credit report from a credit bureau, it cannot include a credit score. So when people say that you've been denied a job because of credit scores, that's simply not true. It is because of what is in your credit report, not your credit score.

Employers are looking to see how you pay your bills. They want to see if there are any bankruptcies, tax liens, judgments or late payments. They are not getting a score and they are not getting all your personal information. The employer credit check does not list your age or date of birth, and does not impact your credit score. This pull is considered a soft, not hard, inquiry. However, on these reports the employer will see your criminal activity—they will know, for instance, that you were arrested for marijuana possession, armed robbery, etc.

Millennials are the ones most affected by employment and credit because they are the ones getting their first jobs. It is in your best interest to make sure you are as credit fit as possible.

Generation X (Ages 35-49)

John's grandmother died. She lived somewhere in the South and he was very close to her. He didn't have enough money to buy a plane ticket and he didn't have a credit card to rent a car because his credit was so bad. As a result, he missed his grandmother's funeral.

"I had never saved the money," he said. "I had a good income, but I couldn't save or keep my credit score up. I missed my grandmother's funeral because I could not afford to buy a plane ticket and it devastated me."

I've heard similar stories far too often.

Gen Xers all have credit scores, and they are more likely to get a new auto or mortgage loan than any other age group. The problem is, more than half of them have credit that is impaired.

Part of the problem, at least from what I've seen, is that the Generation X crowd tends to spend on things they think they should have, but don't need.

Take timeshares, for example. Timeshares are purely a luxury purchase, usually made while already on vacation when you're not thinking clearly and rationally about your budget, and after some persuasive strong-arming. Not to mention a margarita, or three.

Once you've signed on the dotted line, you've committed to return for a week each year or every other year to a place you've already been or may not want to go, and at a rate that would have allowed you to take five people to Disneyland or a hundred other spots you've never seen before.

Why not set aside a budget for a vacation and spend the money how and where you want?

While you're at it, isn't it time to get on top of all the expenses you've committed to, assess the current state of your credit, and do everything you can to get into tip-top credit shape?

Advice for Generation X

Pay down those credit cards

How many credit cards do you have—five, ten, even fifteen? It is amazing to me how many people have 15-20 credit cards, are in massive debt, and feel not only out of control, but hopeless there is anything they can do about it.

In the last couple of years, I facilitated a nine-week class on personal financial management where, among other things, the participants had to cut up some of their credit cards. When I suggest to attendees that they start snipping their cards in half, people initially panic. They will eventually agree to cut up one that they really don't use and that has a small balance they could pay off with their next paycheck. Then, we celebrate having one less card to worry about and move on to the next card. By the end of the course, many of the participants cut up multiple credit cards, even the ones they hid from me or were dishonest about even having. Ultimately, the class is a success.

Why? As people pay down their balances on one, and then another card, by not using them anymore, they feel increasingly relieved.

One gentleman came into one of my classes with a Home Depot card.

"What is the interest rate on your Home Depot card?" I asked.

"Eighteen percent," he said.

"What is the interest rate on your Visa cards?" I asked.

"Three percent on one, and four percent on the other, but I use my Home Depot card all the time."

"Then, why don't you put those transactions on one of your Visa cards?"

"Oh no!" he said. "Every man is supposed to have a Home Depot card."

"Huh?" asked half of the people in the class.

It took him until the very last day, but he finally asked for the scissors and announced, "I am going to cut up this Home Depot card. For the last nine weeks I've been thinking about what you said. I even went to Home Depot and used the card, but I realized it was not smart. Why was I spending eighteen percent on interest when I have the other credit cards at much lower rates?"

Try it yourself with one card.

Once you've stopped using and have paid off Credit Card #1, take that extra money you were paying, and put it on Credit Card #2. Now you get that one paid off; then you go to Credit Card #3. You go with the lowest balances or highest interest rates first.

The thing is, you can't use a high-interest, high-balance credit card when it's been cut up. Better yet, commit to only buying what you can afford, and then create that emergency fund so when an emergency happens you are not struggling. Trust me on this one—emergencies will come, so be smart, and plan. Then, you can sit back and enjoy watching the debt start coming down.

Do not co-sign.

I will go into this in even more depth in the Baby Boomer section, but every time I happen to click past *Court TV*, it seems like some brother is suing his sister or vice versa over a car that one of them agreed to co-sign for, and the other has somehow neglected to pay the car note as agreed. It's the same thing with phones.

Don't help your brother, sister, or friend get a car or a phone and expect him or her to pay you back. From my experience, it's just not likely to happen or if it does, it is rare. Before you decide to co-sign, consider all of the risks and the repercussions that could arise, and probably will arise. For example, if you co-sign on a car for your best friend, you assume all of the risks (missed payments and a decrease in your credit score) and get none of the benefits (your best friend, not you, is driving the car).

Their credit is already bad or they wouldn't need your signature. What will happen is your good credit will take a nosedive.

Did you know, the nicer you are, the worse your credit scores tend to be. Why? Who's more likely to co-sign? Who's likely to do things to help you out of your situation? It's someone who is nice. I'm not advocating that you become a mean, awful person except where co-signing is concerned. I'm telling you to JUST SAY NO!!!

1. Identity Theft

As I mentioned in the Identity Theft chapter, the FTC estimates that ten to twelve million Americans have their identities stolen each year. There's a new identity theft in the US every four seconds, so you or someone you know has experienced some form of identity theft.

While some identity theft victims may resolve their problems quickly, others spend hundreds of dollars and untold hours repairing damage to their good name and credit record. The Identity Theft Resource Center said that many victims spend 300-600 hours to recover their good name and recover financially. You may lose out on job opportunities, be denied loans for education, housing, or cars because of negative information on your credit report. You could potentially even be arrested for crimes you didn't commit.

The very best way to protect yourself is to shred everything before putting it in the trash, protect your ID and personal information, and check your credit report every four months for any inconsistencies or unusual information.

2. Spend Wisely

I know I'm something of an exception, but I advise people not to get a car loan. I will only save up money and buy what I can afford. If I have three to five thousand dollars, that's all I'll spend on an automobile. A car, particularly a new one, is a depreciating asset. No car will go up in value unless it's a mint-condition antique car. It's simply not a great investment. So, if you absolutely have to take out a car note, I urge you to buy it used.

Better yet, spend that money on a house. Yes, I'm a real estate broker and you probably think that I am biased, but real estate typically goes up in value every year. That's a fact. I think the national average is around 4 or 5% and it's the only investment that you can actually use. If you buy stocks or gold or whatever, you can't use them, but you can live and raise your family in a home. I sold a lot of properties where people paid $30,000 thirty years ago and they were able to sell them for $300,000-$400,000. Not only can a small investment become your retirement, you write off the real estate taxes and deduct the mortgage insurance on your taxes. To me, it's a wise investment.

3. Know the value of your credit score.

When you have bad credit, you pay more for the credit you can get. When your credit is good you get the best breaks. You call the shots because creditors want to work with you. They will fight for your business because they know someone with an 825 credit score pays his bills every month, on time. In the end, you will spend so much less for so much more.

According to information from Informa Research Services, Inc., if your credit score is between 760 and 850 and you get a mortgage loan for $100,000.00 (and the APR is 4.02%), your monthly principal and interest payment on a 30-year fixed rate loan is $479.00. If your credit score is between 620 and 639 and the APR is 5.61%, your monthly principal and interest payment is $575.00, about a hundred dollars higher. With a higher APR, you will pay back $106,918.00 in interest (in addition to the amount that you borrowed), compared to $72,326.00 in interest on the loan with the lower APR. Over a 30-year period, you are going to end up spending over $30k more based on your credit score.

The Bottom Line: bad credit is costly.

Baby Boomers (Ages 50-69)

As you might expect, credit scores amongst the Baby Boomer crowd tend to be a bit higher and are typically more stable than that of Generation X, and certainly Millennials. In a perfect world, all the issues of youth have been cleared up. Baby Boomers own houses, and cars, and have learned how to keep on top of the payments for their various assets. Unfortunately, it's not always a perfect world.

1. Circumstances beyond your control.

Sara saved up enough money to open a small clothing business. She had excellent credit. She was proud that she always paid her bills on time and had a credit score in the 800s. From the start of the business, Sara's friend reminded her to get health insurance, especially when business was thriving. Health insurance was expensive, she told him. Besides, she was healthy; she even ran half-marathons. Later that year, she contracted a serious illness. When she became ill, no insurance company would insure her. During that time, she accumulated tens of thousands of dollars in medical bills. Her stellar credit score plummeted and affected her personally and as a small business owner.

Illness, job lay-offs, and unexpected circumstances can wreak havoc on your credit, but thankfully, these situations are typically the exceptions and not the rule amongst Baby Boomers. To combat the sudden loss of one's regular income stream, I suggest staying on a budget while times are good so you have money put away to make sure you can make minimum payments during those inevitable, but hopefully infrequent, lean times.

I also suggest hoping for the best, but preparing for the worst. An emergency fund is inevitable. Start with as little as $200 to $1,000, depending on your monthly income. Each month you should put money into a savings account that is separate and apart from your regular checking or saving accounts. The goal is to save five to six months of your net monthly income. So, if and when an emergency arises, you are more than adequately prepared to deal with it without having to borrow funds, or max out your credit card and watch your credit score drop because your utilization rate is too high. After you recover, begin to rebuild the fund to where it was before the emergency. Keep in mind, by emergency, I mean something that happens unexpectedly and is outside of your control. A trip to Aruba is not an emergency, nor is a sale on designer purses or a new set of tools.

2. Co-Signing

Toni's thirty-five-year-old son had a shiny red sports car repossessed because he didn't make the payments. Now he's mad at her because she will not co-sign for him to get a new car. Tough love? Perhaps, but Toni's credit score is in the 800s and the son doesn't pay his bills on time.

Toni told her son, "I love you, but I am not going to ruin my credit because you don't pay people."

Her son swore up and down that this time would be different.

"What makes me think you are going to pay this car note when you didn't pay any of the others you had?" Toni asked. "You know what, when I wanted something, I would save for it or lay it away. I never bought something I couldn't afford."

Her son was mad for a long time, but Toni told him he'd have to get over it because she wasn't going to put her signature on anything that was going to cause her credit to suffer. Better a lesson learned than Toni, who has always been responsible, paying the penalty for her grown child's poor decision making.

And then there's my fifty-five-year-old friend Lilly:

Lilly's daughter is 30 and can't get an apartment because she's had multiple evictions. The cycle is always the same. She doesn't pay, gets evicted, and lies to everyone as to why. When she applies and is rejected for a new place, Lilly co-signs for a new place, not realizing her daughter has been evicted each time for non-payment. In fact, Lilly had no idea what was going on until she went through a divorce, went to get an apartment, and got denied from every apartment building because she had three evictions on her credit report.

The moral of that story is, of course, and we are talking to the Baby Boomers: Don't become irresponsible for your children.

DO. NOT. CO-SIGN.

What do you do when your son or daughter really needs a car but can't afford it? This may be a bit of a tough pill to swallow, but you're way better off buying the vehicle and giving it to him or her than you are co-signing anything.

From everything I've seen, your son is not going to pay his note, or he's not going to pay on time, and his bad habits will absolutely, positively affect your credit. While you may be sympathetic to the fact that he has three children and doesn't make that much, the bank doesn't care. The finance company doesn't care if he has *five* children. They expect to be paid their $500 or $600 a month, as agreed—by you if you're a co-signer.

I've seen people lose houses because they co-signed or got a mortgage for one of their children who didn't pay as promised. So, if your son needs a car, help him find a car. If your daughter needs a house, help if you can, but do not put your signature on anything that you are financially obligated to pay. That is unless you have the funds and are willing to pay if your son or daughter fails to live up to their financial obligations. Otherwise, not only will your credit be affected, so will your relationship. There's little more damaging than chasing down a family member for money. When they don't pay and you try to repossess that car, they are angry and so are you. However, when the finance company takes it in the middle of the night, it's an entirely different, but much less personal, story.

If you really want to help, help your son or daughter establish a good credit history. If they've already established credit, but it's not as good as they hoped, and you want to help make them more responsible financially, I know of a good book they can read that will explain it all.

You, on the other hand, have your retirement to think about and plan for. Don't let anyone, including your family, get you off schedule.

Your Credit Score and Retirement

Ten thousand Baby Boomers are transitioning into retirees every day. Given the challenges in the economy, some haven't aged so gracefully where their financial situation is concerned. Many Baby Boomers will end up having home loans, car loans, student loans, and credit card balances to pay for in retirement instead of getting to enjoy the fruits of their years of labor.

How does your credit score now factor into how comfortable you'll be upon retirement?

Because most people can't afford to buy a home or pay for college with cash, they depend on a good credit score to get loans. A low score can keep you from getting the best rates, making it more difficult to save now for retirement. Low credit scores often signal too much debt, and debt can prevent a comfortable retirement. Your debt not only affects your current cash flow, it also takes money away from other important goals, such as contributing to retirement accounts and investing.

Reducing the total debt you have now will not only improve your credit score, it will improve your cash flow and financial health so you can finally enjoy being out of the workforce.

Retirees (Ages 70+)

According to the AARP, more than 40% of people in the 65 to 74 age bracket have first, and sometimes second, mortgages on their homes. The average balance on those mortgages is $70,000. Roughly one-third of people aged 65 to 74 use credit cards to pay for basic living expenses (such as groceries and utilities), and have balances that average $8,248.

More than 2.2 million seniors co-signed on student loans, triple the number from 2005. According to the Treasury Department, the number of Social Security checks garnished to cover overdue student loans has risen from six in 2000 to 115,000 in 2012.

For younger people, credit goals are clear—build credit so you can get good terms on car loans and mortgages. If you're a retiree, though, the road ahead is less defined. If you retire with debt, your credit score will definitely matter. A high credit score will allow you to refinance your current mortgage at a lower interest rate, get better loans on a car, lower credit card interest rates, consolidate any remaining student loans, and pay less in insurance. Even if you've planned well and the house and car are paid off, your income will likely be less than what it was during your working years. There could be situations in which you could need some kind of loan. There are also other reasons why retirees need good credit as well.

1. Second Careers:

Some people like to think of retirement as a time to finally do something they love. If that second act means starting a business, you may need start-up funds to get it off the ground. And, as you might expect, lenders will check your personal credit.

2. Saving Money:

Good credit may help you refinance your mortgage when rates drop. It can also help you snag a lower insurance premium if you need to switch providers.

3. Downsizing:

Perhaps you are buying a smaller house? You'll need good credit to get the best rates on a new mortgage. Moving into an apartment? Many landlords check your credit as well.

4 Travel:

Many retirees like to travel. There are many travel reward cards that will help you earn points to pay for those trips or reimburse you for some travel fees—but you usually need excellent credit to get approved for them.

Seeing as good credit can make your life easier and less costly in retirement, you'll want to keep your credit score in maintenance mode.

Tips for keeping up your FICO® Score in Retirement:

1.Make sure you stay on FICO®'s radar with at least one account that's been open for six months or longer.

An open account, available for use, will likely be reported to the bureaus on a monthly basis, regardless of whether there is any activity on the account.

2. Use your credit cards from time to time on gas or groceries.

You can eventually become unscorable if you let your accounts lie dormant so long that your issuer closes them. Any accounts you've closed in good standing will fall off your reports in ten years, and if paid-off mortgages and car loans have fallen off too, you could eventually become invisible to FICO® and therefore not qualify for new credit.

3. Remember to pay your bills on time every month and use no more than 35% of your available credit, as low credit utilization will boost your FICO® score.

4. Keep your credit safe.

Seniors are at risk for identity theft because they may not be checking their transaction history regularly via online banking, or pulling their credit reports every year. That gives ID thieves plenty of time to open accounts in their victim's name and tarnish his or her credit before the victim finally applies for credit and gets rejected.

Above all else, remember, it's your obligation to understand the value of your assets and your good credit.

Here are some prime examples why:

When I was a credit and housing counselor, an older man came into my office looking for some advice. He had a house he had paid off in full and he was on Social Security, making $600 a month. His roof started leaking, so he went to a mortgage broker for a home equity loan. The broker charged him a $10,000 (this is not a misprint) broker fee and about $5,000 in additional junk fees. They paid his real estate taxes and they arranged to have his existing roof replaced. In the end, the man only got $1,000 cash on a $30,000 loan. Worse, the roofer took off with the money and never replaced the roof. The poor man came in saddled with an interest rate of 14%, and a payment of over $500 a month. He was left with $100 out of his $600 Social Security check to pay the rest of his bills. When he came to see me, he had just lost his home in a mortgage foreclosure sale.

Unfortunately, I couldn't help him get his house back, but I did do the only thing I could do: I called the mortgage broker and let him know that I was aware of his schemes and would report him to the proper authorities.

The poor man he fleeced, however, had to go live with one of his children. Had he known he had very good credit when he went in to see the mortgage broker, he could have gone anywhere and gotten a loan for a few thousand to replace his roof, and would have paid less than $50 a month for that new roof. He would also still have his home.

While this is extreme, it's by no means the only tragic story I've encountered amongst retirees who were either misinformed, or trying to do the right thing for their children. One of the most common financial missteps I've seen is older people who have transferred the deed to their houses to their children.

Smart, right?

I'm not a lawyer, but if you transfer your house to your daughter or your son, know that your son or daughter now owns your home. If your son or daughter gets upset with you, he or she could sell what is now their home and force you out. They can also mortgage that property and squander the money. They don't have to tell you, because they own the property. Unfortunately, I have seen it happen more times than I care to write about.

I know an older woman who put her grandson's name on her big, beautiful house shortly after his father died of a sudden heart attack at the age of 45. This trusting grandmother, who was close with her only grandchild, hadn't considered that he might one day have a drug problem and need money, which he got by mortgaging that house. They had a dispute, he moved his girlfriend in, he kicked his grandmother out, and changed the locks. She had little recourse but to leave the home she'd purchased with her late husband 45 years ago.

While you may think this could never happen to you, there's no accounting for other people in your children's or grandchildren's lives who may not be such a stellar influence. So, instead of signing over your deed, I suggest you leave it in a will. People don't do this, because they've heard somewhere that they should transfer the deed because they don't want their kids to pay inheritance taxes when they die. This is not necessarily true. I always advise my clients to contact an attorney for the best way to proceed.

All retirees should remember that a high credit score is like good health: invaluable.

Moreover, think of good credit as a marathon you plan to win, not a sprint where you have nothing left to finish the race.

CHAPTER EIGHT

Game Changers
Until Debt Do Us Part—Marriage, Divorce and Credit

Michelle had a lot of debt. Marcus had somewhat less, but more than he should have. When they got married, their debt became one. Together, they made a spreadsheet and wrote down the names and balances of all their credit cards. They concentrated on paying off one card at a time, and paid the minimums on the others. Both reported they actually enjoyed the process of watching their debt go down, and the satisfaction of growing up and learning the process of being responsible together.

This is an ideal scenario—a couple who were aware of each other's financial situations before they tied the knot, worked together to pay off debts, and increased each of their credit scores as a married couple.

It's not a typical scenario, I'm afraid.

How often do you think your average twenty-two-, twenty-three-, or even thirty-five-year-olds divulge their financial situations as part of their courtship? Seeing as there's a 60% chance of getting divorced, and the number one reason for divorce stems from disagreements over money, the answer has to be *not often enough.*

From my experience, talking about financial issues is of paramount importance to a healthy marriage at any age or time period in your life. It is also one of those topics people shy away from discussing, mostly out of embarrassment. It shouldn't be. I don't hesitate to advise couples to talk about debt, credit, and that all-important FICO® score with each other. I mean, isn't it preferable to deal with what may well be a harsh reality on the front end, instead of waiting until you get into the marriage, and then find out your spouse has bad credit?

As I've mentioned, numerous couples have sat down before me, ready to buy a house, until we run the credit. The scene unfolds from there in the same awkward, awful way—I have to explain that I can only get the partner with good credit on the loan, which inevitably turns out to be the one who makes half the income of the other. In marriage, two may become one symbolically, but not for the purposes of their FICO® scores. As a result, their blissful dream of a home with a white picket fence gets tempered by harsh financial reality.

If you are both young people, one of the two of you is likely to have some credit issues. In fact, 75% of the couples I deal with have an issue where both names can't go on the mortgage. The solution for avoiding this scenario is simple: talk about your bills and credit history, then check your credit together. I believe credit reports should be a mandatory part of pre-marriage counseling. Granted, it may take a bit away from the romance, but think of all the heartache it will save later. It shouldn't be shameful or embarrassing—in fact, you will go into this significant union honestly. If this is the person you are going to marry, and it turns out he can't get a credit card because of judgments or tax liens, doesn't that start off your life together on a dubious note?

My advice to couples is simple: reduce the amount of money that you plan to (over)spend on your wedding and put that excess money towards your debt, especially if those accounts include judgments and tax liens. By paying off these negative and damaging items on your credit report, you and your new spouse will be in a better place, literally and financially, when you decide to purchase a new a home or automobile.

If your spouse or fiancé has bad credit, you should help them rebuild their credit score. If you and your spouse or fiancé both have bad credit, you can rebuild your credit together as a couple. This foundation will help you develop good money management habits and stick to them. If you love each other, you can help each other achieve your shared goals more quickly and without unexpected obstacles. If you know one or the other of you has a problem, you can work together as a team to fix credit, bring the score up, and improve the health of your relationship from the outset. One way this can be done is by adding the spouse or fiancé with the impaired credit as an authorized user on your credit card. By doing this, you will help your spouse re-establish a credit history. Authorized user accounts are included in a credit report and can be considered when making lending decisions. However, an authorized user has no responsibility for the payment of the debt.

For couples with good credit, I recommend each have cards in their individual names and get some cards in their joint names. I also recommend you keep your total debt as a couple to 35% of your combined line of credit. It's not that I don't believe in happily ever after, but to ensure smooth sailing along the way. And, just in case things don't go as planned, you both maintain control over your all-important personal credit and credit score.

Divorce

Steve's estranged wife had bad credit before they married and she never did anything to improve it. Now they are separated. Hoping for a rec-

onciliation despite this and other warning signs, he co-signed for a line of credit for her. She hasn't bothered to pay. She won't pay the mortgage on the house they owned together, either. The mortgage company won't even call her anymore, they just call him because she's made it clear that since her credit is already messed up, she simply doesn't care and has no intention of paying anything. Steve, who used to have an 800 credit score, is stuck paying all the bills. He wanted to protect his credit so he paid every month until he just couldn't afford to do it anymore. As he is unable to keep up with all the expenses every month and has been late for the last few months, his credit score has dropped to the low 500s.

Sadly, too many marriages end in divorce. While I would never encourage anyone to go into a marriage believing it is going to fail, are you prepared financially if it does?

Despite all the ominous indicators, Steve certainly wasn't.

In my experience, many people suffer financially as the result of divorce. When a couple gets married, it is important that both spouses maintain at least one individual account in his or her name. If each spouse has not established credit cards in his or her name, he or she will have no credit if the marriage comes to an end, especially if it ends acrimoniously. If you added your spouse as an authorized user, remember to remove the spouse from that account. Otherwise, the ex-spouse could continue to charge on the account and not be financially responsible for the bill. I've also seen husbands and wives go through ugly divorces where both worked, but the court decreed that the husband had to pay a $20,000 American Express bill, for example. Because it was a joint account, and it was being reported on both of their credit reports, he paid it late out of spite. As a result, the ex-wife's good credit took a nosedive. I've certainly seen women do the same to their husbands.

If you have joint accounts, and you get a divorce, a judge can order you responsible for that account, but the judge can't order the bank to take the spouse off the account. If your ex doesn't pay, your credit drops too.

Unfortunately, that's why we need to talk about credit and divorce.

It's also the reason you need to think worst-case scenario during the good times. By this, I mean keeping your financial situation under control and your credit in line for all the right reasons.

1. Make sure there is a credit card in each of your names. Not just joint accounts.

2. Understand what you are and are not signing for in terms of car notes and mortgages.

3. Use your credit responsibly by keeping your debt at or below 35% of your credit balance.

If your debts are low, both of your credit scores will remain high. It is also easier to pay them off and walk away without that debt.

If you have maintained a solid financial bond, but your marriage doesn't work, then your chances of getting out of the marriage without the collateral damage of credit problems is not only possible, but likely.

When Divorce is Imminent

1. If you have the funds, pay off as many of these credit cards as possible so you don't have the debt.

2. Gather all your credit card statements, mortgage information, any kind of loan agreements, and decide who is going to be responsible for the various obligations.

For example: "Hey, I'll take the American Express, and you take these two. You make less money than I make so I am going to take the $25k and you take the two $5k and pay those."

3. Contact creditors and have the other party removed as an authorized user. Close all joint accounts.

Assuming you have credit cards in each of your names separately with the other as an authorized user, you will each retain a credit card or two.

4. Keep in mind that even if the divorce decree mandates that your spouse pay a jointly held account, it still does not release you from liability.

Don't assume that the other spouse is making the payments. Sometimes divorce brings out the worst in people and revenge is taken in the form of not making the payments. At the very least, the former spouse typically does not care how missing payments will impact the other person, or his or her credit report.

5. Pay off as many of the joint accounts as you can before you get a divorce. If you are unable to do that, try to turn the joint accounts into individual ones.

For example, you can transfer a balance from one credit card to another that is in the name of one spouse, and then close the joint account.

6. In the divorce decree, spell out what happens if your spouse misses a payment on joint debt.

For instance, he or she must notify you in advance so that you can make the payment and avoid damaging your credit.

Most of all, do what you can to retain your wits where the financial aspects of your marriage dissolution are concerned. I realize this is much easier said than done, but do what you can to avoid the headache and heartache of paying the additional price for years to come.

Second Marriages

Randall, a successful doctor, was 55 years old when he married his second wife, Mary. To protect his two children from his first marriage, he established a trust and named the children as beneficiaries. That way, the two million in assets he'd earned before his second marriage would go to the children when he died. Mary would inherit whatever he made from the date of their marriage on.

Their union was long and successful. However, Randall suffered a heart attack and died suddenly at the age of 65. Mary decided to sue for a share of the money he'd put into the trust. Because every state has a law that entitles a surviving spouse to a portion of the estate even if the will or a trust says otherwise, and she did not expressly waive her right to the money in a prenuptial agreement, Randall's children lost a third of the inheritance their father had earmarked for them.

Marriage today is more complicated than ever. Second marriages can be that much more so. A new bride may well find herself married to her husband, but also to his alimony and child support payments. A groom might become an instant father if his new wife has children from a prior relationship. Because more than 40% of marriages are second (or even third) unions for one or both of the partners, you need to approach a second (or third) marriage like you would any other financial agreement: very carefully.

While most couples pay close attention to the wedding budget, many fail to hash out the more important financial issues that will impact their relationship. Who owns the assets accumulated before the marriage? Who is responsible for child support from the children produced in a prior marriage? If you are getting married for the second time, there is absolutely no excuse not to ask, *what is your financial health?*

In fact, the question should be followed up with a number of more specific questions:

How much do you make in a month?

Where are you financially?

What is your credit history?

What's your credit score now?

Are we going to buy things together?

The list goes on…

If it is your second marriage, and you plan to keep everything that is yours and live in your house but she is going to do the same with her assets, that's one thing. But, if you are going to sell your houses, buy a house together and co-mingle your assets, everything should be spelled out. Second marriages typically include children and stepchildren. Have you had a discussion about who is going to pay for their college educations? The subject may not be romantic, but addressing these issues ahead of tying the knot may well be the smartest, healthiest thing you can do for your relationship.

My best advice for second and subsequent trips down the altar is this: discuss the past, present, and future of your financial lives together in detail. Then make a plan that outlines everything, create a budget, and enjoy your new life together.

Financial To-Dos for Second Marriages:

Before you get married, you and your fiancé should discuss all aspects of your financial situations, including the following:

Credit History

Have you ever been late on payments, or had any judgments against you? Have you *ever* declared bankruptcy?

Debts

How much do you owe on credit cards? What other debts do you owe?

Assets

Your assets include annual salary and earnings, plus the value of your homes, cars, investments, and retirement plan funds.

Obligations from a previous divorce

Reveal any child support or alimony payments you are required to make (including how much), as well as any disability, life, health or long-term care insurance that your settlement says you must keep in effect. You should also let your partner know if your ex-spouse has rights to any of your future retirement plan earnings.

In addition, you will need to discuss and decide who is responsible for debts incurred before the marriage, whether you will share assets earned by one of you, and how you will meet financial obligations from a previous marriage.

You will then need to decide whether you will draw up a prenuptial agreement.

A "prenup" is particularly important if you are:

1. Bringing significant assets into the marriage.

2. Will be inheriting a business or other assets in the future.

3. Have children from your previous marriage(s).

Protecting Your Assets

Typically, people are older and wealthier than the first time they married. As a result, you will likely bring more into the marriage and have more to protect. You may also want to protect assets you'll earn during the marriage. A prenuptial agreement will ensure that your assets will continue to remain separate from your spouse's, that the spouse cannot claim a portion of your assets if you divorce, and vice versa.

Protecting Your Children

If you have children from a prior marriage, and want your assets to pass to them when you die, a prenuptial agreement is very important. Unless your spouse specifically waives his or her right to the assets in a valid agreement, he or she may claim a portion of your estate when you die. If you're like most and want to provide for your spouse, but preserve assets for your children, you may want to consider a Qualified Terminal Interest Property, or QTIP, Trust. This trust lets your surviving spouse enjoy access to the assets during his or her lifetime, but enables those assets to pass to your children upon the surviving spouse's death.

After the Wedding

Not only do you need to discuss your financial situations before the wedding, you should examine your long-term financial plan once you are married, including:

Insurance

Do you have enough? Do you need to increase your life and disability insurance? If you are 50 or older, you should consider long-term care insurance. Chances are, you or your spouse may need such care in the future.

Beneficiaries

Many newlyweds fail to update the beneficiaries on their life insurance policies, trusts, company retirement plans, and IRAs. If you're not on top of this, you could leave money to your ex-spouse and neglect your current spouse!

Wills

A new marriage means you need a new will.

Assets

Your assets may require a post-nuptial agreement or necessitate a waiver to your prenuptial agreement. It's always a good idea to speak with a lawyer and find out.

Marriage can be one of the happiest moments of your life, but it does have financial implications. Proper planning is more important than you may realize.

CHAPTER NINE

Trips and Falls
FICO® Score Killers

We've discussed a number of bad things you can do to your credit. This chapter is devoted to the very worst things, not so affectionately known as the FICO® Score Killers.

They are:

- **Bankruptcy**
- **Tax Liens**
- **Mortgage Foreclosures**
- **Short Sales**

Any and all of these issues will cause your credit score to fall in varying degrees, depending on your prior credit profile. More important, these FICO® Score Killers will remain on your credit report for up to ten years, so you will feel their effects in both the short run and for years to come.

Let's take a look at each one in detail:

1. Bankruptcy

David and Francis dated for two years before they married. He worked for a small construction company and she taught kindergarten. Both loved to travel, dine out, and buy expensive clothing and accessories. Each of them had several credit cards on their own, but after their mar-

riage they managed to accumulate an additional fifteen credit cards together. When they received the credit card statements each month, they could only afford to pay the minimum payments because they had so many cards. In addition, they still had two car payments and a student loan to pay. Within a couple of weeks, each was unemployed—the company he worked for went out of business and her job was eliminated because of budget cuts. Because they had little to no savings and a lot of debt, they decided to file for bankruptcy protection. They were relieved. A year later, they both had jobs that paid them more income than before. They even saved enough money for a down payment on their first home. The problem—no bank would approve them because of the bankruptcy. They were told that they would have to wait years before they could get a mortgage.

Bankruptcy is defined as a legal proceeding involving a person or business that is unable to pay outstanding debts. The bankruptcy process begins with a petition filed by you (known as the "debtor") or on behalf of the creditors. All of the debtor's assets are measured and evaluated. Once this is determined, the assets are used to repay a portion of outstanding debt. Upon completion of the bankruptcy proceedings, the debtor is relieved of the debt obligations incurred prior to filing for bankruptcy.

While it may seem good to be relieved of your debt obligations, particularly when they've piled up to the point where you feel like there's no other way out, you should do everything you can to avoid this situation from occurring.

Why?

Nothing affects your credit more than a bankruptcy, or for as long. A bankruptcy is considered the most negative mark on your credit report and will severely impact your FICO® score for years to come.

How much does your credit score drop if you have a bankruptcy?

The simple answer is it could drop as much as 200 points. The impact a bankruptcy will have on your credit score depends on your entire credit profile. For example, someone with excellent credit will experience a huge drop in their FICO® score. On the other hand, someone with poor credit is likely to experience a more modest drop in his score because there isn't as far to fall. The more accounts included in the bankruptcy filing, the more of an impact on your score. No matter where your credit score started, however, your ability to get new credit will be all but nonexistent. In addition, a bankruptcy will show up on your credit report for up to ten years.

Bankruptcy filings in the United States fall under one of several chapters of the Bankruptcy code:

Chapter 7: involves liquidation of assets.

Chapter 11: involves company or individual reorganizations.

Chapter 13: involves debt repayment with lowered debt agreements or payment plans.

Question: Chapter 7, 11 and 12 bankruptcies can remain on my credit report for 10 years from the date filed; Chapter 13 bankruptcies can remain for 7 years from the date paid.   True or False?

Answer: True

Chapter 11 and 7 bankruptcies will remain on your credit report for ten years from the date FILED. Chapter 13 bankruptcies (wage earner programs where you are making payments to a bankruptcy trustee) can remain on the public record and your credit report for seven years from the date paid. This is important because most people think Chapter 13 bankruptcies have to be removed seven years from the filing date, which is incorrect. It normally takes three to five years for a Chapter 13 to discharge. That's when the seven-year period begins. Because the cap on all bankruptcies is ten years, most

Chapter 13 bankruptcies remain on the credit report for a full ten years, just like Chapter 7 bankruptcies.

Before you file for bankruptcy, contact Consumer Credit Counseling Services or another nonprofit organization to see whether there is a reasonable hope of paying off your debts. If you do opt to file for bankruptcy, know that all the individual accounts included in the bankruptcy will show up on your credit report for seven years and the bankruptcy will show up for up to ten. The only thing you can do to help, however incrementally, is to make sure the accounts that are not a part of the bankruptcy filing are not being reported with a bankruptcy status.

Beyond that, all you can really do after you file for bankruptcy is take small steps to start rebuilding your credit. For instance, apply for a secured credit card with a low credit limit to start the rebuilding process, as soon as possible.

I hope the message here is clear: while many of us will face the issue of declaring bankruptcy, it should always be your last option.

2. Tax Liens

Peter was a successful real estate agent. He was the top producer in his office. Then, the real estate market crashed. The problem: Peter spent and spent and did not save any money to pay his income taxes. Since he is considered an independent contractor, his taxes are not withheld, and he is responsible for paying the income taxes himself. Because he had such a profitable year, he owed the IRS $10,000. Peter could not pay his taxes and the IRS filed a tax lien against him. His pristine credit and high score were severely impacted.

A **tax lien** is a lien imposed by law upon a property to secure the payment of taxes. A tax lien may be imposed for delinquent taxes owed on real property or personal property, or as a result of failure to pay income taxes or other taxes.

A federal tax lien gives the IRS a legal claim to your property for the amount of an unpaid tax debt. Filing a Notice of Federal Tax Lien is necessary to establish priority rights against certain other creditors because the government is usually not the only creditor to whom the taxpayer owes money. A lien informs the public that the U.S. government has a claim against the property, and any rights to the property of the taxpayer. This includes property owned at the time the notice of lien is filed and any acquired thereafter.

A lien will affect your credit rating, so it is critical to arrange the payment of your back tax bill as quickly as possible.

It's too late—I already have a tax lien.

If you're reading this and you're already in this situation, do everything you can to arrange to get your back taxes paid. Once you do, I have one bit of very important advice. The IRS announced in February of 2011 (2011 Fresh Start Initiative) that it would withdraw the tax lien if it is paid in full AND the taxpayer requests a withdrawal. So, if you have a tax lien, and you pay it, all you have to do is fill out the form I've included as Appendix B and send it to the federal government. They will remove the lien from your credit report.

Even if you haven't paid off the tax lien entirely, you can still fill out the form and ask them to remove the lien from your credit report. Seeing as unpaid tax liens can stay on your credit report indefinitely, it's certainly worth a try. Section 605 (a) (5) of the FCRA states, "Liens (other than paid liens) may be reported as long as they remain effective."

As you can see, it's only three boxes. It says the taxpayer or the taxer acting on behalf of the taxer believes withdrawal is in the best interest of the taxpayer and the government. Even if you haven't paid off your debt, there's no harm in trying. If you have paid your back taxes, they must remove the lien if you send this form. It's important to note that if you are granted a "withdrawal," this will remove the public Notice of Federal Tax Lien and assures that the IRS is not competing with other creditors for your property. This does not relieve you of your obligation, however. You are still liable for the amount due.

Do not confuse the 10-year statute of limitations for tax debt with the credit-reporting period for tax liens. The 10-year statute of limitations for tax debt refers to the amount of time the IRS has to enforce its lien (i.e. seize your assets). It has no effect on the credit reporting periods or how long a paid or unpaid tax lien can remain on your credit report.

If you simply pay the tax lien and don't send the form in, paid liens remain on your credit report for seven years from the date paid. This includes liens that have been settled for less than you owed.

Why allow such a bad mark on your credit to remain when it doesn't have to be there?

3. Foreclosures

A **Foreclosure** is a legal process by which a lender or the holder of the Promissory Note terminates the borrower's rights in the property through a court order. The court sets up a date by which the borrower can redeem the property by paying off the entire loan balance (including foreclosing expenses). If the borrower fails to pay off the loan balance, the lender takes possession of the home. A mortgage is a security document that allows the borrower to keep title to the property, which is being used as collateral for the loan. A lien is placed on the property in the event the borrower does not make the agreed-upon monthly payments. Once the borrower becomes delinquent on those payments, the lender could foreclose or take back the property from the borrower through legal action.

According to RealtyTrac®, the nation's leading source for comprehensive housing data, mortgage foreclosure activity (foreclosure filings, default notices and bank repossessions) throughout the nation, with a few exceptions, continues in its downward trend.

4. Short Sale

Sheila, a recently divorced mother of two, purchased a home in an up-and-coming neighborhood. Unfortunately, the neighborhood has yet to come up, and it actually went down. Sheila always struggled to make the monthly mortgage payments and began to fall behind when the real estate taxes almost doubled. She decided to sell her dream home and move her family into an apartment. The Realtor® informed her that the value of the home was thousands of dollars less than what she owed on the mortgage loan. The bank agreed to allow her to sell the home in a short sale or for less than what was owed. The bank agreed to write off the difference. The house sold. Her credit score dropped almost a hundred points.

A **Short Sale** is a sale of real estate in which the proceeds from selling the property fall short of the balance of debts secured by liens against the property. The bank or mortgage company (lien holder) then agrees to release their lien on the real estate and accept less than the amount owed on the debt. In plain speak, this means the homeowner cannot get the amount of unpaid principal he owes the lender by selling the property, and the lender concedes to taking the loss.

Short sale agreements do not necessarily release borrowers from their obligations to repay any shortfalls on the loans, unless specifically agreed to between the parties. However, in some states, like California, legislation was passed to preclude deficiencies after a short sale is approved. The same is true of lenders on first loans and lenders on second loans—once the short sale is approved, no deficiencies are permitted after the short sale. A short sale is often used as an alternative to foreclosure because it mitigates additional fees and costs to both the creditor and borrower.

While it may appear to be a better option than foreclosure, alternatives such as short sales and deeds in lieu of foreclosure (the borrower deeds the property to the bank, the bank takes possession of the property, and the borrower is relieved of all financial responsibilities) are all "not paid as agreed" accounts and are considered the same by your FICO® scores. These options or alternatives to foreclosure are no better or worse for your FICO® SCORE.

Why?

While a borrower's willingness to work with the lender should have a positive effect on his/her credit risk, one out of every two borrowers who experienced a short sale defaulted on another account within two years. Additionally, a majority of consumers with short sales have some other issues with mortgage delinquency. Consumers with a reported loan modification (a process where the terms of the mortgage are modified or changed from the original terms of the contract agreed to by the lender and the borrower; for example, the interest rate may drop from 6% to 4% and the monthly payment would be lowered and become more affordable to the borrower) statistically perform worse in repaying their credit obligations.

October 2009 to October 2011, was a period of unprecedented mortgage distress. While it is true that short sales represent slightly better risk than foreclosures, they do not perform well enough to receive a more positive treatment in the FICO® Score. The results closely match earlier studies of the risk associated with short sales and other events of mortgage stress.

From a FICO® Score perspective, bankruptcy, tax liens, foreclosures and short sales all fall into the same class because they correlate with exceptional riskiness. Based on the data, consumers with short sales perform no better than consumers who have a severe delinquency (90+ days past due) or a collection on file. In comparison, only about one in every fifty borrowers with a score in the high 700s will default on one of their credit obligations. Lenders depend on this information to separate out good from bad credit risks when they are deciding to issue loans and credit.

Among other things, the analysis above looks at the impact of mortgage delinquencies on your credit score. But what if we examined the consumer's subsequent payment behavior on bankcards alone, a credit obligation far removed from their mortgage obligations?

There remains a strong link between poor bankcard payment behavior and consumers who experience a mortgage stress event. In fact, for all of the events in question, the bad rates observed are at least twice as risky when compared to the total population.

Other FICO® Score Killers

While perhaps not quite as fatal in terms of your FICO® score, be aware of these additional pitfalls, issues and black marks on your credit:

Collection/Charged-off Accounts

Question: A collection account can be reported for seven additional years if sold to a different collection agency.
True or False?

Answer: False

If your account is sent to a different collection agency because the first one could not collect, that does not, however, start a new seven-year reporting period.

If an account that was charged off is later paid in part or in full by you, the consumer, the reporting period of seven years from the charge-off is not extended by the payment (per section 605 (a) (5) of the FCRA). This is known as re-aging a debt. Collection agencies used to do it all the time. Your collection account is now five years old. The collection company sells it to another company and it starts the seven-year period over again. That's why they amended the Fair Credit Report Act to protect consumers from this practice.

Re-aging a debt is now illegal—this occurs when a creditor or collection agency reports a collection or delinquent account as newer than the actual "FCRA Compliance Date." This allows the negative information to remain on your credit report for longer than permitted by the FCRA. The FCRA Compliance Date must be reported within ninety days of the trade line or account being placed in your credit file (per section 605 (a) (4)).

A collection account remains on your credit report for seven years from the initial missed payment that led to the collection. Keep in mind, if you enter into a repayment agreement with the creditor or the collection agency, it may be treated as a new account that has its own seven-year period (per section 605(a) (4) of the FCRA).

If your account is placed for collection with an outside collection agency, and you make a repayment arrangement with the collection agency but fall behind on the payments, it can begin a new reporting period.

Do not make payment arrangements with collection companies if you cannot keep them.

The FCRA allows credit bureaus to report negative information longer than 7-10 years in the following conditions:

If it's for a credit application greater than $150,000

If it's for a life insurance policy with a face value greater than $150,000

If it's for employment purposes and the salary is greater than $75,000

One important thing to keep in mind is that the older the negative information, the less of an impact it has on your FICO® score.

Inquiries

Every time someone runs your credit, your credit score drops. Remember, there are two different inquiries. There's a hard inquiry and there's a soft inquiry. A hard inquiry occurs when you initiate credit, such as when you apply for credit cards. If you go to five different department stores today and apply for their credit cards, your score is going to drop five different times and it could be about three to five points each time. The soft inquiries occur when a credit card company offers you a pre-approved credit card or an employer runs your credit. No one else sees these inquiries but you when you check your credit. You're not actually applying for credit. Someone is just looking at your credit report. As I've mentioned, inquiries remain on your credit report for two years, but they're only factored into your score for one year.

The exception is when you apply for a car loan, mortgage, or student loan within thirty days of scoring; then your credit score is not affected at all.

If you are shopping for a car loan or home loan during a 45-day time period, after the first thirty days, the auto loan inquiries would be counted as one inquiry, and the mortgage loan or student loan inquiries would be counted separately as another inquiry. This is because they represent three separate searches for credit.

If you are concerned about the impact of shopping for an auto, mortgage, or student loan, simply do your interest rate shopping in a reasonably short period. Do your homework ahead of time to decide which companies to approach for quotes. Such planning also should make the loan rates easier to compare, since the quotes will come only a few days apart.

The FICO® Score does NOT consider:

Consumer disclosure inquiries - requests made by consumers to obtain a copy of their individual credit report in order to check it.

Promotional inquiries — requests made by financial institutions in order to make pre-approved credit offers.

Account review inquiries - requests made by lenders to review existing accounts with them.

Employment inquiries - requests from employers.

Insurance inquiries — requests from insurance companies.

How much does a credit inquiry impact a FICO® Score?

In general, inquiries have a small impact. Typically, a single inquiry can lower a FICO® score by less than five points. The exact impact will again vary based on each person's unique credit history. Inquiries can have a greater impact if consumers have few accounts or a short credit history.

Why does a credit inquiry affect the score?

Research consistently shows that consumers who are seeking new credit accounts are riskier than consumers who are not seeking credit.

Student Loans

The FCRA does not govern the amount of time defaulted student loans can remain on your credit reports. The amount of time is actually governed by the Higher Education Act. Defaulted student loans can remain on your credit report for seven years from the date they are paid, seven years from the date they were first reported, or seven years from the date the loan re-defaults.

Credit Accounts

Negative information remains for seven years from the initial missed payment that led to the delinquency. In other words, seven years from the last scheduled payment—seven years from the date that the payment was supposed to have been made.

According to section 605 (c) of the FCRA, the seven-year period "shall begin, with respect to any delinquent account that is placed for collection (internally or by referral to a third party, whichever is earlier), charged to profit or loss, or subjected to similar action, upon the expiration of the 180-day period beginning on the date of the commencement of the delinquency which immediately preceded the collection activity, charge to profit and loss, or similar action."

Section 605(a) (4) of the FCRA sets forth the method for determining the date that starts the seven-year period. This section requires any party that reports such accounts to a CRA (credit reporting agency or credit bureau) to provide the "date of delinquency" that the CRA must use to calculate the seven-year period.

Active positive information can remain on your credit report indefinitely. (If an account is closed that has been positive, it can be removed after 10 years.) This is not a requirement of any federal or state law but is instead the policy of the credit bureaus. There is no requirement to remove anything on your credit report that is positive.

Overview:

Chapters 7 and 11 bankruptcies remain for 10 years from the date filed.

> **Completed Chapter 13 bankruptcies remain for 7 years from the date paid, and 10 years if not completed.**
> **Paid tax liens remain on file for 7 years from the date released (paid).**
> **Unpaid tax liens can remain on file indefinitely.**
> **All judgments remain for 7 years from the date filed.**
> **All consumer-initiated inquiries for the purpose of obtaining a loan and/or benefit remain on the file for 2 years.**
> **Paid collections remain 7 years from the date of last activity.**
> **Delinquent child support obligations can remain for 7 years.**
> **Late payments remain for 7 years from the date of occurrence.**
> **Repossessions and foreclosures remain for 7 years.**
> **Settlements can remain for 7 years from the date of the original delinquency.**

What does all this really mean?

Really, it's pretty simple. Do everything you can to avoid bankruptcy, tax liens, foreclosure, or any of the other FICO® score killers. Let's say for example, you apply for, run up, and end up in collection on ten credit cards by the time you're 23. By 24 you've declared bankruptcy. It will take years before you are able to raise your credit score and qualify for credit.

That may be too long a time.

You may get married during that time period. You may start a family. You may want to buy a house. Life is going to be all the more challenging if you can't even get a credit card. (Although you may be able to get a secured credit card to rebuild your credit.)

And, while there's no statistical correlation between a low credit score and poor job performance, tell that to the employer who is looking at your credit report along with a host of other applicants. Who is he going to hire—you or the other candidate with the clean report? Who would you hire? While one study actually found that the more disagreeable a person you are, the better your credit, it's hardly information you can, as they say, *take to the bank.*

Wouldn't you rather be able to approach the bank, lenders, and that employer with a credit report that reflects you in your best possible light? Understanding and, hopefully, avoiding the pitfalls discussed in this chapter will help you do just that.

CHAPTER TEN

There's No Such Thing as a Shortcut
Credit Repair

Life after bankruptcy and/or foreclosure is undeniably tough. If you have experienced a bankruptcy or mortgage foreclosure, the first thing to remember is that you are not alone and that you can rebuild your credit. Granted, it is not easy, but if you are willing to put in the time, you can do it.

I suggest you take the following steps:

1. Commit to changing your past behavior and create good money management skills.

2. Create a budget.

Make a realistic budget that you can and will live by in order to monitor all of your spending, and which designates money to its rightful place (or creditor).

3. Apply for one or two secured credit cards.

Remember to keep the balance as close to zero each month as possible.

4. Create an emergency fund.

Until you have saved three to six months of your total monthly expenses, continue to put money into this account, separate and apart from your other checking and saving accounts. It is better to open the emergency account at a different bank altogether, and with no ATM bankcard.

Just as you did not get into this situation overnight, you will not get out of it overnight either. The key is patience, persistence, and perseverance. Though things will be challenging, there are steps you can take to start rebuilding your credit so that you can eventually regain your standing and qualify (at a decent rate) for credit cards and other loans.

There are also significant missteps that should be avoided on the path to regaining your financial footing. The biggest and most grievous? Signing up with a less than reputable credit repair company.

During my stint as a housing and credit counselor I met with many clients who'd paid up to $5,000 to have their credit "fixed," only to discover that they'd not only overpaid for services they could have done themselves, but were sold a bill of (sometimes illegal) goods.

What is a Credit Repair Company?

According to the Credit Repair Organizations Act (CROA), the federal law that defines how credit repair companies must do business, a credit repair company is actually referred to as a credit repair organization (or CRO). A CRO is anyone who "Sells, provides or performs a service, in return for the payment of money or other valuable consideration, for the express or implied purpose of improving a consumer's credit record, credit history, or credit rating."

The exception to this is nonprofits that perform these duties. Banks and credit unions are not considered CROs either. So, any for-profit organization that isn't a bank, that sells services promising to help improve a consumer's credit report, is considered a CRO. Ideally a CRO does the following, according to the main provisions of the act (effective April 1, 1997):

1. You must be given a dated, written contract that explains the services that will be performed, any guarantees about services, how much it will cost you, and the date by which the service will be completed.

2. You have the right to cancel the contract, without penalty, within 3 business days after you sign. Your contract must also explain how to cancel.

3. Before you sign a contract with a CRO, they must give you a statement that explains your credit reporting rights under state and federal laws. The company must get your signature on that document and keep it on file for two years.

Additional state laws may also require credit repair firms to be licensed or bonded.

It is illegal for a CRO to make any statements that are untrue or misleading, or to advise you to make a statement that is untrue or misleading to a credit reporting agency or a credit grantor. They can't tell you to lie about accurate, but negative, information. It is illegal to advise you to alter your identification or alter the identification of your credit report in order to remove or hide negative but accurate information in your credit report. And yet, we are inundated with billboards and advertisements promising to solve every credit issue you could ever have:

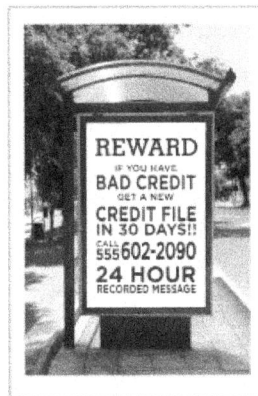

I'm sure you've seen an ad like this, or heard one of the following claims:

"Credit Problems? No Problem! 100% Guaranteed!"

"Create a new credit identity! Legally!"

"We can remove bankruptcies, judgments, and liens from your credit report."

Unfortunately, I've seen far too many of these credit repair businesses charge hundreds or thousands of dollars to outright scam desperate people in their darkest financial hours. These companies prey on consumers with damaged credit by making it sound as if it is possible to erase bad credit.

Credit Repair Company Rip-offs

Question: A credit repair company can <u>legally</u> remove negative information from my credit report that is accurate.

True or False?

Answer: False

Credit Repair Companies cannot legally remove bad credit unless it is incorrect or past the seven-year period.

While many credit repair companies claim to have knowledge of little-known provisions or loopholes in the law that give you the right to remove negative information from your credit file, this is not accurate. There are no little-known legal provisions they know that you can't find out for yourself.

The Fair Credit Reporting Act, the federal law that governs credit reports and credit bureaus, grants you the right to dispute any information in your credit report that you believe is incorrect, incomplete or outdated. Credit repair companies will often advise you to dispute all of the negative information on your credit reports, even if it's true. They will instruct you to send letters or forms disputing the same information every day for weeks. The goal is to jam up the system so your request will not be verified and the information will be deleted from your credit report.

What these companies won't tell you is that if the credit bureaus can later verify that the information in your credit report is accurate, that same information can be re-inserted into your credit file.

They also neglect to tell you that the CRA does not have to initiate an investigation at all if the CRA believes the dispute is frivolous or irrelevant (Section 611 (a) (6) of the FCRA).

The Fair Credit Reporting Act states the following: "A credit reporting agency or a credit bureau must assume a consumer's dispute is bona fide unless there is evidence to the contrary. Such evidence may constitute receipt of letters from consumers disputing all information in a file without providing any allegations concerning the specific items in the file or of several letters in similar format to indicate that a particular third-party, i.e. credit repair operator, is telling consumers to dispute all items in a file regardless of whether that information is known to be true."

If you send a letter claiming something on your credit report isn't yours, and the credit bureau looks at it and decides it is frivolous or irrelevant, they simply send you a letter saying, "We're not doing anything because we believe your claim is without merit." So, if they think that you're working with a credit repair company and all you're doing is disputing everything, now you've paid good money for nothing. Worse, you may have brought bigger problems upon yourself because you're saying everything negative is not yours, which is not true.

According to the Consumer Data Industry Association, the trade organization of the credit reporting agencies, about 30% of all disputes are submitted by credit repair organizations. Many of the items that credit repair companies get removed would be removed anyway if consumers tried to have them removed on their own, instead of paying a fee.

Credit Company Scams

A few years ago, I saw the sign from a few pages back on a telephone pole, and I took it down.

Knowing this had to be a scam, and a huge one at that, I called the 800 number. Just as I expected, I got a recording that instructed me to send in money—$89 to be exact. Wanting to know what kind of bait-and-switch these people were running, I ordered the material.

For my hard-earned dollars, I soon received a two-page letter that explained to me how to create an entirely new credit identity. Never mind that the process, which is known as file segregation, is entirely illegal.

File segregation, which can land you in a lot of trouble, is a process by which you try to separate or segregate your original credit file from the new file you create using a Taxpayer Identification Number (TIN) or an Employer Identification Number (EIN), a form of a TIN number, instead of your Social Security number.

A TIN or EIN is much like a Social Security number, but is used by the IRS to track individuals and businesses for tax purposes. When you file your tax as a business, then you have to have an identification/account number, which is the way the IRS identifies you.

An unscrupulous credit repair company will advise you to establish a TIN or EIN— because these numbers have nine digits, just like a Social Security number. They tell you to give your company your name; my company would be named Trent Pettus, for example. You then get a tax identification number that looks like a Social Security number. You use that tax identification number in place of your Social Security number. You go to a department store and apply for a credit card under your company name, which just happens to be your own name. Since your tax ID number looks like a Social Security number, nothing comes up on your "clean" credit report. Theoretically, you get a credit card, the department store credit department is none the wiser, and you have just established a new credit identity.

The problem?

A TIN or EIN is not a substitute for your Social Security number. It's also against the law to use them as such.

It is a federal crime to lie on a credit application so:

1. If you are using that TIN or EIN in lieu of your Social Security number, you are being dishonest.

2. It is a federal crime to misrepresent your Social Security number, so if you are using your TIN or EIN in place of your Social Security number, that's another felony you've committed.

3. You have given the TIN or EIN to the IRS on false pretenses. You are not using it for business purposes; you are giving it because you are trying to create a new identity. Yep, that's another crime.

As if charging you for this bit of illegal advice isn't enough, another method, which credit repair companies seem to be using more and more, is to sell you Social Security numbers stolen from deceased people, senior citizens and children.

Child Identity Theft

Child identity theft occurs when a child's identity is used by another person for the imposter's personal gain. While the perpetrator is often a family member or someone known by the family, it can also be a stranger who targets children, because of the length of time between the fraudulent use of the child's information and the discovery of the crime.

There are two scenarios in which child identity theft typically occurs:

1. A parent or family member may have destroyed his or her own credit or driving record. He or she may even have a criminal record. This person uses the Social Security number of their child in order to obtain credit, a driver's license, or employment.

2. An identity thief steals your child's Social Security number. He or she either uses it for their own gain or sells it to an unscrupulous credit repair company. The credit repair company then sells it to the person who needs new credit. This person then "becomes" your child.

This can happen more easily than you might expect, because credit issuers do not always verify the age of the applicant. The information on the application is typically taken at face value and credit issuers rarely request sufficient proof of identity. The credit bureau has no way of knowing that the application is fraudulent, and the age of the applicant for a credit bureau becomes "official" with the first credit application. So, if the first application states that the applicant is 26, the credit agencies will believe that person is 26 until a dispute is filed and proven.

Since none of the credit card bills will come to the rightful address of the owner of the Social Security number, child identity theft victims typically find out many years later that there's a problem when they:

- Are denied credit, a mortgage, or a loan for a vehicle or college tuition.
- Are unable to open a bank or checking account.
- Receive collection notices.
- Are denied tenancy, or utility or phone service.
- Are denied a driver's license or renewal.
- Are let go from a job or continually or inexplicably denied employment.
- Start receiving bills or credit cards they never requested.

- Are denied SSI or Welfare services.

And, by far the most disturbing:

- Are arrested for a crime they never committed.

It is typically ten to fifteen years from the time the information is stolen that this crime is discovered. By that point, the paper trail is cold and damage to the child's credit record can be great. The original fraudulent accounts that were opened at whatever store or credit card company may have gone through several hands. This makes it difficult to track down the original application and transaction records. The criminal may have used the information until the credit history is destroyed and he or she can no longer get credit with that identity.

Even when the identity fraud is discovered earlier, it can be difficult, not to mention frustrating, to prove that the child (or young adult) did not open the accounts. Parents often have to prove that the child is a minor, and indeed their dependent. They are placed in the position of being the primary investigators and have the ultimate responsibility of restoring their child's identity.

Scary as all of this sounds, there's truly no need to panic if you happen to get something in your child's name. For instance, if you receive a pre-approved credit card offer in your child's name, it is most likely a legitimate marketing tool sent by an affiliate of the bank where you opened a college fund for your child.

If you are concerned, however, you should contact the credit bureaus and request a credit report for your child. If you are told there is no credit report, that is good news. A credit report should not exist until that child's first credit application as an adult. From now on, make it a habit to check your children's credit reports, or lack thereof, every four months when you check your own. If somebody has done something to any of your family's credit, you're going to look and you're going to find it within four months, and they're not going to be able to do too much damage.

Report Credit and Credit Repair Fraud

If you find that you or your six-year-old has been the victim of this type of identity theft, report it to the police, first and foremost. Next, you will have to contact each of the three bureaus. Then, you will have to notify the credit issuers so you can clear your records. Each of the credit bureaus has departments set up where you can report identity theft, but be aware it takes time and patience to get things cleaned up. It may take three or four years, even as an innocent victim.

Do you need an attorney?

That depends on the offender or person who is using the information. If the offender is a parent or relative, or if this is a case that could be tied in to a custody or divorce issue, it may be necessary to involve a family law attorney. This is especially true in joint custody cases. If you have joint custody of the child, timing is critical. If you fear that the offending parent might run *off* with the child, seek the advice of your attorney as to timing, legal actions that might assist you in protecting the safety of the child, or the need to involve child protective services.

If the offender is a relative, you might find that law enforcement is reluctant to get involved. Be patient, but persistent when requesting a police report for identity theft.

Each case is unique. However, in many cases an attorney is not able to do anything you cannot do for yourself. There are always exceptions to this rule, so I suggest that you contact itrc@ idtheftcenter.org (mailto:itrc@idtheftcenter.org) or toll-free at 888-400-5530.

Do you need a new Social Security number?

The Social Security Administration (SSA) has very strict standards about granting a new Social Security number. In most circumstances, you will not need to apply for a new Social Security number. If you believe you or your child can benefit from such an action, you can contact the Social Security Administration by calling (800) 772-1213 or by going on line: www.ssa.gov (http://www.ssa.gov/).

Credit Repair Company Rip-Offs

If you have been ripped off, not by identity theft but by a credit repair company claiming to be able to fix yours, report it to the police and the district attorney as well. Most of the time these companies are pretty slick, though. Typically, they'll have you do all the legwork so nothing sticks to them, just to you.

Before the mortgage foreclosure crisis, there were mortgage brokers who also called themselves credit repair "specialists." When someone with questionable credit wanted to buy a house, they would challenge everything and get the credit bureaus to remove a lot of the negative accounts or trade lines. As a result, their client's credit score would go up. The mortgage broker would get you a pre-approval, but the transaction had to close before the negative information was later verified by the creditor and re-inserted onto the credit report by the credit bureau.

I was at a closing with a client, not knowing that's what he had paid to have done. The lender pulled the credit the morning before closing, and denied the loan because they said that the credit score had dropped.

Having no idea what was going on, I was shocked and certain there had been a mistake until my client admitted that he'd paid over $1,000 to someone who promised he could "clean up" his credit.

What they neglected to promise, or tell him, was that the information would go right back onto his credit report as soon as the credit bureaus investigated the claims. Unfortunately for him, the investigation was completed before the closing.

No matter how much they "do for you" or charge you, the credit repair companies never put their names on any documents. Your name is on everything. So, you're the one that's being untruthful. If anything goes wrong, you are the one who will be charged with mail fraud because you sent in a signed letter stating that an item or items on your credit report aren't yours when, in fact, you knew they were. If you do it over the telephone, you can be charged with wire fraud. Even if you didn't write the letter the credit repair company has you send in, you signed it.

As a result, you don't have a whole lot of people complaining about being taken in by unscrupulous business people, because they know that they were trying to get away with something dishonest themselves.

How do you tell the difference between a legit repair company and a rip-off?

There's a federal law that governs credit repair companies. As mentioned earlier in this chapter, it is called the Credit Repair Organizations Act (CROA). Before you sign a contract with a credit repair organization, they have to give you a written contract that explains the services they will perform, any guarantees about the services, how much it will cost, and the date by which the services will be completed. You have the right to cancel the contract without penalty within three business days.

Now, here's the thing: most legitimate credit repair companies will not charge you in advance, but I've never heard of a credit repair company not getting their money up front.

THE RACE FOR GOOD CREDIT • 133

That, right there, violates this act.

Many states also have laws regulating credit repair companies. If you have a problem, report it to your local consumer affairs office or to your state attorney general. You can also report credit repair fraud to the FTC. Although the FTC can't resolve individual credit disputes, it can take action against a company if there is a pattern of possible law violations.

File your complaint online at ftc.gov/complaint or call 1 877-FTC-Help.

There are no special tricks or shortcuts.

The simple fact is that credit repair companies do not have any special tricks. They cannot create a new identity for you. This is illegal. They cannot remove bankruptcy or liens unless the time period has passed. They cannot erase bad credit unless the items on your record are either incorrect or outdated. There are legitimate credit repair companies that help consumers rebuild their credit, but they are not only few and far between, they provide services that consumers can and should do themselves.

Now, going back to that sign I took down. I wanted to find out who was behind the 800 number and the false promise of creating a new identity so I could make sure they were driven out of business.

I turned the information over to the proper authorities, who were able to put him out of business. Basically, he was telling people how to create a new credit identity, illegally.

The long and short of it

There is no easy fix for bad credit, and, as we have seen, there can be innocent victims as a result. It took you years to get into this situation, and it is not going to take you two or three days or three months to get out of it. I believe you do not need a credit repair company to help you. I would say 99% of them are rip-offs. Most of them will charge you $50 to $90 a month to get items off your credit report that you can do yourself. Many of the items that are ready to come off will come off anyway after the seven-year reporting period has passed.

It may take you up to three years, but if you are persistent and do what you need to do, you are going to see your credit score go up and your credit profile improve. More important, you are going to feel better about it because you are headed in the right direction and didn't pay thousands of unnecessary dollars, or inadvertently break the law.

In the next chapter we'll talk about specific steps you need to follow.

CHAPTER ELEVEN

It's How You Play the Game

Credit Repair and Restoration

*F*red was paying the minimum on his credit card by auto-deduct
every month. When his financial situation became more fluid, he
sent in a request to increase the amount so he could pay off the card
more quickly. Assuming the change had been made, he didn't think
about the lack of an email confirming his new deduction amount.
As it turned out, there had been a glitch in the system and his auto-
deduct had instead been cancelled. Five months later, he got a notice
from the credit card company cancelling his credit card for nonpay-
ment. He was shocked, since he always paid all of his bills on time, or
so he thought. When he checked his credit, his high 700s rating had
dropped to a 580.

Clearly, Fred should have insisted on an email confirmation, but
had he monitored his credit every four months, he'd have noticed the
problem much sooner, saving himself time, money, and the headache involved in straightening out the mistake.

Mistakes like this one occur all too often—car payments lost in
the mail, mortgage payments that are mailed in on time only to sit
on someone's desk for a week, and payments that come in just before
"processing day" and are thus counted as late. Sadly, the bottom line,
as far as the credit company is concerned, is the same:

Whether it was your fault, or the result of factors outside of your control, a late payment equals a negative mark on your credit report.

Now Fred, in the example above, had his credit card for years and had never been late, so he was able to talk to a manager who could look at his history, determine that he had a legitimate issue, and help reverse the damage to his credit. But what about those of us who haven't quite maintained the best habits? Those of us who, before reading this book, were feeling desperate enough to approach a credit repair company in the hopes they might have the magic answers to help get us out of a mess of our own doing? A company that, contrary to what they may have told you, didn't have any tricks or magic formulas that allowed them to remove accurate and timely information from your credit report. Once again—if a credit repair company tells you otherwise, hold on to your wallet or your purse and run as fast as you can. There are **no** little-known provisions in the law that only they are aware of.

Let's look at the steps you can (and must) take for repairing and restoring your credit report, and thus, your credit itself.

The Credit Repair/Restoration Process
1. **Get a free copy of credit report at annualcreditreport.com.**
2. **Review credit report for mistakes.**
3. **Check identifying information in credit report.**
4. **Review all trade lines/credit accounts.**
5. **Examine the collections and public records.**
6. **Dispute all errors.**

Let's review each of these steps in depth:

Step 1: Get a Free Copy of Your Credit Report.

As we've discussed, since 2004, all Americans have had the right to receive one free credit report from each of the three national credit bureaus every 12 months. All of the three largest national credit bureaus house over 200 million consumer credit files. Collectively, they hold more than 600 million credit files that can be claimed each year. To get a copy of your free report, log on to www.annualcreditreport.com or call 1 877-322-8228. This is the only authorized source under federal law. As mentioned before, the other "free" sites will charge you a fee to monitor your credit.

Step 2: Review Credit Report for Mistakes.

Once you have a copy of your credit report in hand, look at it and see if there are any issues. If there is anything that is outdated, incorrect, or missing, you need to dispute that information. Once you correct the error on your credit report, your score will increase.

Step 3: Check Identifying Information in Credit Report.

Check identifying information in all credit reports. Is your name spelled wrong? Is the address correct? Sometimes you'll find they've transposed the Social Security number at one of the credit bureaus and maybe someone else's information is on yours, or they have an incorrect address for you, or they have some misinformation that also could be an indication of identity theft. Your name may be Elizabeth, but on some applications you put Beth, so now it's showing up as Beth and Elizabeth or Liz, so you want to make sure that all information is consistent. If you ever applied for credit with a significant other when you were together, it will show up. Your mother's address or your employer's may well show up, too. Those things don't affect your score, but you want to make sure that all the information on your credit report is consistent and correct.

Step 4: Review All Trade Lines/Credit Accounts.

Make sure all these accounts are yours. Twenty percent of all credit reports have at least one major mistake. A mistake that could cost you up to twenty-five points. This step is crucial because if you are trying to get a mortgage, you need a 620 credit score and you have a 600, a mistake like this could keep you from getting a mortgage.

Equally as important, you could get different interest rates on a loan, which could be tens of thousands of dollars more over the life of that loan. So instead of getting 4% percent you're now getting 5%. We don't have as many subprime loans as we used to, but there's a prime loan for people with good credit and subprime loans for those with not-so-good credit. A prime rate could be 4-5%, while a sub-prime rate could be 6-8%. If you are looking at a $100,000-$200,000 property and most of your interest is paid up front, it could be a thirty to eighty thousand dollar difference over the life of your loan. When we talk about a car note, if the finance company is financing your car loan, your interest rates probably are going to be closer to 20% if not over, but if you go to your credit union and get a car note for 3%, that's a huge difference—and it all depends on your score.

Step 5: Examine the Collections and Public Records.

Once again, make sure that everything there is accurate. If there's a judgment and it's not yours, it's going to have a huge effect on your credit score. Remember, tax liens can be removed if they've been paid. Even if they're not paid, you may be able to get them removed. If you're on a payment plan, the IRS may be willing to remove the lien as long as your money's being debited out of your account.

Common Credit Report Errors:

1. Wrong name or address.

2. Information belongs to someone else with the same name.

3. Duplicate information on the same account.

4. Balances are still showing on accounts that are paid.

5. Accounts reporting as delinquent that were never paid late.

6. Incorrect credit limits are shown.

7. Incorrect dates of activity.

8. Accounts included in bankruptcy showing still owed.

9. Court records such as bankruptcy or judgments are wrongly associated with you.

10. Foreclosures that never happened.

Step 6: Dispute the Errors.

Once you review your credit report and find incorrect, incomplete, or outdated information, you need to initiate a dispute with each of the credit bureaus. You can dispute the information by using their dispute forms, write your own letter, or dispute the item online at their website. If you have more than four disputes on your credit report, don't dispute everything in one letter.

Once again, DO NOT LIE. Whatever you say, make sure it's true. Don't try to change information to make it more favorable to you. If you now go by Liz Smith instead of Elisabeth Smith, don't say you're not that person. You have to be 100% honest. Also, look at all the information carefully; sometimes you may not recognize a collection agency because the original creditors may have sold your account to another collection agency. Look at the information and the dates, not who is handling the account.

The credit bureaus have thirty days, once they get your dispute, to initiate what they call a re-investigation. Whatever they find out, within five days after their investigation, they have to send you a letter saying whether they were able to verify the information, and that credit bureau must update your report to reflect the change. If they made a correction, then they have to send you a copy of your updated credit report within five business days of the completion of the investigation—this report does not count as your free annual credit report. If you so request, the credit bureau must also send notices of any deleted information to anyone who received your credit report for any purpose in the last six months, and for the last two years for employment purposes. In other words, if Macy's requested a report and there was a mistake, they have to send information saying there was a mistake and "here's a new copy of the credit report." Now, if they don't do it within thirty days, then you can insist they remove the item. The credit bureaus have an extra fifteen days if you send them any additional information during that 30-day period, or if you dispute an error after receiving your free annual credit report.

Under FCRA, if the credit bureaus do not meet the 30-day deadline for verifying disputed information, they must delete the information. You should note however, that they can re-insert it later if the information provider verifies that it is accurate and complete. Unfortunately, credit repair companies usually fail to tell their customer this vital piece of information before or after they take your hard-earned cash.

Do Not:
Alter or try to change your identity.
Make up a fictitious story.
Dispute any information that is 100% accurate.
Most important, be patient.

While it may feel like debt piled up quicker than you could ever have imagined, or that your bankruptcy or foreclosure came out of nowhere, the truth is, unless you had some unforeseen illness or un-avoidable life circumstance, bad little habits can have big, ugly consequences. However, everyone makes mistakes and faces adversity. Winners don't give up; they make the necessary changes and finish the race strong.

With some perseverance, patience, and a commitment to improve your spending, saving and debt repayment habits, you can too.

CHAPTER TWELVE

The Race Isn't Over Until You've Crossed the Finish Line

Six Proven Strategies

No matter how far you've fallen, you can brush yourself off, start over and, with time, rebuild your credit. I have seen people who had credit scores in the low 400s build them back up to the high 700 range. I've run into people I was working with ten years ago who've told me, "Great news! My score is now holding strong at 780. Remember, it was 500?"

What did they do to improve their credit and keep it that way?

For one thing, they didn't work with credit repair companies. For the sake of argument however, let's say, best-case scenario, you do go ahead and spend the money and they do get some of the negative information off of your credit report. As we discussed earlier, in some cases, the deleted information may be re-inserted if it is determined that the items were later verified by the credit bureau. What they can't and won't do is help you change the behaviors that got you into trouble in the first place. In fact, if you don't adopt better habits, research shows you're going to go back and start charging up your cards, missing payments, and maybe even having that car repossessed again.

I say you need to fix your mistakes so you understand the impact of your former behaviors. In the process, you'll develop new, better habits for handling your money, credit, and financial future. The good news is there isn't anything a credit repair company can do that you can't yourself, it'll cost you a whole lot less, and it won't be nearly as hard as you think.

That is, if you implement and take to heart what I call the Six Proven Strategies for Improving your Credit.

Six Proven Strategies:
1. Check Credit Report for Mistakes

We went through the process in the last chapter, so for the sake of brevity, I'll simply say go to **annualcreditreport.com**, make sure all the information on your credit report is accurate, complete and not obsolete, and dispute any errors by following the instructions provided in Chapter Eleven.

2. Pay Bills on Time

Once the credit report side is sorted out, you need to sort yourself out. Make a list, figure out what needs to be prioritized, and be sure you pay at least the minimum on every credit card and obligation, every month. It doesn't matter whether you owe $10 or $1,000, you made a commitment to pay for what you've purchased and the debt needs to be addressed every month, on time. It's important to remember that your credit will not take a hit for paying the minimum, but it will take the same hit for a late payment, regardless of how much you owe. Late is late, so get your bills paid on time.

3. Pay Down the Balances on your Credit Cards

We all want to have little or no debt and the very best credit score. To do so you need to keep the balances as low as possible, preferably less than 35% of your available credit limit. FICO®'s research revealed that consumers with credit scores of 785 and up (those in the top 25% of credit scores) have an average of seven open credit cards. Of those seven, an average of four credit cards or loans have balances. They keep low balances on the credit cards. They use only 7% of available credit. Ninety percent of them have had one late payment and one in one hundred have an account that had gone into collections.

4. Do Not Open a Number of Accounts in a Short Time

In other words, you only want a limited number of people running your credit at any given time because your credit scores drop with each inquiry. People have a tendency to go shopping, put in multiple applications to take advantage of discounts and incentives. Many end up getting denied because their score instantly drops fifty to sixty points, depending on the number of credit applications submitted.

When I have clients who are first-time homebuyers, one of the things I tell them is, "Listen to me carefully, at this point no one gets your Social Security number until you close on your house." I've seen it happen too often; people finance furniture before settlement, their credit score drops, and they don't get the house because their debt to income ratio is suddenly way too high.

5. Get a Secured Credit Card

If you can't qualify for an unsecured credit card, you can still get a secured credit card through your local bank or credit union. Adding new, positive information by paying your secured credit card on time, over time, is probably the strongest credit reference that you can have on your report. Once your credit improves, limit yourself to two or three credit cards at the best interest rates possible. As I've mentioned, these cards should not be department store cards, which tend to have high interest rates.

6. Do Not Co-sign for Family and Friends

Co-signing for family or friends can damage relationships and kill your credit score. Be mindful of this fact: if your friend or family member is not responsible when it comes to paying his or her other debtors, don't be surprised when they do not pay you or honor the debt owed to the creditor for whom you co-signed. My advice: Just say no.

Cash Is King

In addition to the **Six Proven Steps**, I believe it's vitally important to use cash whenever possible.

Why?

There's a big psychological difference between using cash and pulling out a credit card.

Years ago, a friend of mine used to go to Atlantic City and play Blackjack. I asked him to teach me how to play too. So for months, during lunch, he came over and we ate and played Blackjack. One Friday night, we drove to Atlantic City. I put a $100 bill down, hit, and won. The high roller seated next to me told me I should put down $200 the next time. I kept winning to the point where I had close to $80,000 in chips. I, Trent, who was so careful with my money, started throwing out $1,000 or $5,000 chips. I would have never put $5,000 worth of cash anywhere, but it felt like funny money. I even put a $10,000 chip down once. I had so much money that people started crowding around me.

But, as we all know, when you sit at a table too long, you start to lose. As the evening wound down, I started putting down $5,000 chips and losing again and again. I got a little smarter and started putting down hundreds, only to lose those too. I was smart enough to grab a handful of chips and ended up with $5,000, but I lost probably $75,000.

Yes, I came out ahead, but the moral of the story is if the chips were cash, I would have never bet such huge numbers. Credit cards can be much the same way. Would you actually buy that watch or pair of Ugg boots for $300 if you had to peel the bills from your wallet?

When I was in college, and started getting credit card bills I couldn't pay, I had no idea what to do. My roommate came up with the (not at all) brilliant suggestion that I simply send the bill back. Believe it or not, that's exactly what I did—that is with a nice note scrawled across the front saying, "Please don't send this back to me."

They responded with another copy of the bill.

The point here is when you use a credit card, it feels like it's not cash coming out of your pocket. If you use actual cash, or even a debit card, you are much, much less likely to spend frivolously since the money is coming directly out of your pocket or your account.

You need a credit card if you're travelling and need to stay in a hotel or rent a car, but not if you're just going to the mall. If you're going to go shopping, allow yourself a set amount—say $500. Take that $500 and have a good time, but if you get to the store and they're having a great sale on shoes, and two pairs are $550, you have a decision to make. With the credit card, you're way more tempted to go ahead and buy both. Never mind that you'll lose the sale "price" with the interest you'll accrue making payments. With cash, you'll buy what you can actually afford and stay within the shopping budget you set for yourself.

And While We're on the Topic of Budgets...

Bottom line—the most important step you can take to improve your credit for the long haul is to become disciplined enough to manage your spending wisely. In addition to everything you are doing to repair your credit, it's crucial that you create not only a budget from this point forward, but also a savings plan and an emergency fund.

Budget

When I was a housing and credit counselor, the one thing my clients seemed to have in common was poor money management skills. They did not think about what would happen tomorrow if they spent too much money today. They would go out and spend money on a Friday, not thinking about the fact that the rent was due on Monday. Money came in and they spent it, not taking into account their fixed expenses, much less the items they wanted but couldn't necessarily afford.

Sit down, go through your monthly expenses, and write them down. Compare them against your monthly income. Once you've determined that you've covered everything, including at least the minimum payments on your credit cards and other loans, then you can determine how much discretionary income (or fun money) you have remaining. Only then is it time to go shopping—and only for those clothes or shoes you have the money in hand to buy.

Savings plan

And what about those bigger expenses like, say, a vacation? Set aside a certain amount of money every month, ahead of time. It's infinitely more relaxing to lie on a beach, soaking up the sunshine, when your trip is bought and paid for than it is to pull out a credit card knowing you're going to have to figure out how to pay for it, with interest, when you get home.

Emergency Fund

An emergency fund is crucial for those times when your car breaks down, your heater stops working, or your roof springs a leak. I suggest you put away at least $1,000 and build on it for these unexpected but inevitable emergencies, in a different bank or in a different account of a bank that you normally go to. Do not get an ATM bankcard or checks for this account, as it's too tempting to dip into this money. By setting up this account, you won't find yourself having to finance an emergency expense by using a credit card, or worse, asking someone else to lend you the money when it happens.

I realize that asking you to not only budget, but also to set aside money for the future, may be a tall order, but it can be done. You will have to work at this. You will have to be consistent. It will take time, and patience, and perseverance. It very well might take you two or three years, but the rewards of having achieved good credit will far outweigh the stress and frustration of the years of bad habits you've overcome.

What about those of us who've done our best in the past, kept a budget, and saved up for the unforeseen, but still come upon tough financial times?

The fact is, no matter how responsible you are, you can run into hard times. While there is no magic formula for keeping your credit pristine when things go poorly, there are some steps you can take to keep your credit score at a relatively stable place.

Never hide from creditors

If you don't open mail, or take their calls, the result can be resentment, anger, and much worse. I started my real estate business in the middle of the recession. In truth, there were times when I wasn't bringing in enough to cover the rent. Instead of hiding from my landlord, I went to him, looked him in the eye and told him, "Here's my plan. I may be able to give you $1,000 or $2,000 now but I cannot pay the full amount this month. When I can, I will get current immediately."

Which I did.

Not only did my landlord never evict me, he trusted me when it happened again—more than once. My credit stayed solid, and so did my relationship with my landlord.

The bottom line is, if you owe someone money, his call is the most important call you can receive. Do not hide. Take that phone call and see what you can work out. More than likely, you'll be amazed at what people are willing to do if you are open and honest with them.

CHAPTER THIRTEEN

Winning the Credit Race
The Power of Behavior

Test Your Credit Knowledge

Remember that quiz you may have huffed and puffed your way through at the beginning of this book? Compare your answers and let's see how much more credit fit you've become now that you're well on your way to being credit fit.

1. The highest FICO® credit score is 950.

True or False?

2. In order to generate a credit score, I need at least one credit account that has been open for 6 months or longer.

True or False?

3. A low credit score can keep me from getting a certain job or promotion.

True or False?

4. My payment history affects my credit score more than any other factor.

True or False?

5. Co-signing for family and friends is usually a bad idea. If I co-sign, I agree to share full responsibility for payment of the debt.

True or False?

6. A credit repair company can <u>legally</u> remove negative information from my credit report that is accurate and not outdated.
True or False?

7. The 3 major credit bureaus are Equifax, Experian, and TransUnited.
True or False?

8. The only site where I can get a free credit report each year as mandated by the federal government is <u>www.freecreditreport.com</u>.
True or False?

9. The Fair Credit Reporting Act (FCRA) is designed to help ensure that all information in my credit file is complete, accurate, and not outdated.
True or False?

10. I should review my credit report at least once a year.
True or False?

11. Race, gender, and employment history are factored into my credit score.
True or False?

12. Negative information remains on my credit report for 7 years from the date of the missed payment that led to the delinquency.
True or False?

13. A collection account can be reported for 7 additional years if sold to a different collection agency.
True or False?

14. All judgments, whether paid or unpaid, remain on my credit report for 10 years from the date filed.
True or False?

15. Unpaid tax liens can remain on my credit report indefinitely.
True or False?

16. Chapter 7, 11 and 12 bankruptcies can remain on my credit report for 10 years from the date filed. Chapter 13 bankruptcies can remain for 7 years from the date paid.
True or False?

17. A 30-day late payment made today is not as bad as a 180-day late payment made 6 years ago.
True or False?

18. When I get my credit card balances to zero, I should close them.
True or False?

19. If I apply for credit cards at Macy's and The Gap today, my score will drop 2 times.
True or False?

20. All auto, student loan, mortgage-related inquiries made within 30 days of scoring are completely ignored.
True or False?

21. Identity theft is one of the fastest-growing crimes in the country.
True or False?

22. According to a recent FTC study, 20% of all credit reports contain mistakes.
True or False?

23. Credit Scoring is a system creditors use to determine whether to give me credit.
True or False?

24. There is a strong correlation between a low credit score and poor job performance.
True or False?

25. Carrying high student loan debt will hurt my credit score.
True or False?

Now, check your answers against your original set of answers:

1. False

850 is the highest FICO® Score.

2. True

A credit score is generated by having at least one credit card that has been open for six months or longer.

3. True

Forty-seven percent of employers run credit to determine whether they're going to hire or promote you.

4. True

Whether you pay on time, as agreed, your payment history constitutes 35% of your credit score, making it the most important factor that affects your score.

5. True

If you co-sign, you share responsibility for repayment of the debt and the risk that the bill will not be paid by your friend or family member.

6. False

A credit repair company cannot legally remove anything from a credit report that is accurate or not obsolete.

7. False

The three credit bureaus are Equifax, Experian, and TransUnion.

8. False

-www.annualcreditreport.com is the only place that you can get a free credit report. The other "free" sites actually charge you a fee to monitor your credit report.

9. True

The Fair Credit Reporting Act is designed to help ensure that the information in your credit file is complete, accurate, and not outdated.

10. False

You can and should get three reports for free each year, one from each of the three major credit bureaus. Stagger them and get one every four months to protect yourself from mistakes and identity theft.

11. False

Neither race, gender, nor employment history are factored into credit scores.

12. True

Seven years.

13. False

This practice, called re-aging a debt, is no longer allowed. The Fair Credit Report Act was amended to outlaw this practice.

14. False

A judgment comes off your credit report seven years from the date it was filed.

15. True

Tax liens are typically taken off after about 15 years, but they can remain indefinitely.

16. True

17. False

If you are late this month it is going to have a bigger negative effect than if you were late 3 years ago. So, the more recent the delinquency, the worse it affects your score.

18. False

Thirty percent of your credit score is made up of the amount of your available credit that you have used (referred to as your credit utilization ratio). Keep your balances as close to zero as possible. The more credit you have, but aren't utilizing, the better your score will be in this area.

19. True

Every time someone runs your credit, your credit score drops. If you go to two different department stores today and apply for credit cards, your score is going to drop two different times and it could be about three to five points each time.

20. True

All student loan and mortgage-related inquiries made within 30 days of scoring are completely ignored. The scoring system is designed to recognize when you are rate shopping, looking for the best interest rate for one loan. The system knows when you're shopping for a car, a mortgage, or a student loan. After the 30-day period, any inquiries made within the next 45-day period will be treated as only one inquiry for each of the three types of loans.

21. True

According to the FTC, as many as nine million Americans have their identities stolen each year.

22. True

All the more reason to check your credit report three times a year.

23. True

24. False

Unfortunately, too many employers run credit during the pre-screening process to determine if they are going to hire you, even though there is NO correlation between credit and job performance. None.

25. False

You can have high student loan debt and still have a good credit score. Just make sure you're making your student loan payments on time. Remember, your payment history accounts for 35% of your credit score.

And the winner is…?

How much did your score change compared to the first time you took this quiz? Substantially, I hope. Whether you got 100% this time around or you just learned a lot more than you once knew about credit, it's all about improvement, increased awareness of the importance of your credit score, and changes in your behavior.

I wrote this book because information is knowledge, and because the educational components about credit seemed to be missing for so many people. When I think about the clients I saw when I was a housing and credit counselor, and so many of the prospective home-buyers I meet each day, I'm struck by the commonalities: poor money management skills, lack of knowledge about how to budget, overspending, instant gratification, and little idea about the consequences of their financial decisions. I wanted to clear up all the fallacies and misinformation so any reasonable person who may have learned it wrong, or hasn't been taught about the importance of credit scores in the first place, can start correcting his or her mistakes.

We all feel the need to keep up with the Joneses—particularly when Mr. or Ms. Jones has a sporty new luxury car and a house on the hill. It can take years to mature enough not to compare the car or home you own to theirs, but to realize the more important issue is how well each of you can afford what you're driving or calling your home. For some of us, it takes enormous restraint to learn how not to buy that feel-good pair of shoes or make some other emotional purchase, sometimes at the expense of coming up short on the mortgage or the rent. While it is often the case that these bad fiscal habits are passed down from one generation to the next, the curse can be broken with some knowledge, diligence, and some effort on your part.

The Power of Behavior

If you have a goal to own a house, buy a car, or start a new job, you now know that your behavior can adversely or positively affect the outcome. Bad credit can prevent you from getting that house, and it can directly affect the price you pay over the life of a loan, keeping you from being able to afford other things you may want or need. Worse, a bad credit score can result in a monthly payment that you can't afford in the first place.

My greatest hope is that this book has given you the information and tools you need. If you're starting out, you can establish good habits right off the bat. If you've made mistakes, now you know how to substitute good habits for whatever bad habits you've already developed. You have control over your behavior. It's simply a matter of instituting changes, being diligent about maintaining them for the long haul, and recognizing that by making these changes you will feel better about yourself. You are gaining control and empowering yourself. When you realize you are in control and you've got some power, you start to feel good about yourself, and find that it actually feels better to resist buying that new pair of shoes, at least until you can afford to.

As of today, make a solemn oath to yourself to start paying your bills on time. After that, be sure to follow the **Six Proven Steps** for improving your credit. The change will be incremental, but if you do all these things, your credit score will definitely increase.

More opportunities will open up from there.

This morning, I happened to see a familiar commercial where a woman walks into a car dealership looking proud and confident because she knows her credit score and what it means for her. Before the salesman can give her the runaround, she says, "I have a great credit score and am expecting the best deal."

That's the mentality I want for you.

When you walk into a car dealership, or a bank, and see they are going to charge you all manner of fees, points, or an unreasonable interest rate, I want you to feel empowered to say, "Wait a minute. I pay my bills every month on time so I am an ideal person to lend to. I've got a credit score in the high 700s or low 800s. You need to give me your best deal because I can walk out of here and go anywhere."

Chances are, they'll give you their best deal.

Your good credit is not only your blue ribbon, but also your own personal platinum card with no credit limit. And I am confident of this: Now that you've read this book and digested its contents, if you follow the steps laid out for you, you will get a fresh wind to finish your race stronger than ever.

Appendix A

(We refer to this Act throughout the book and without it there would be no book. Also, I always ask those in my seminars to become familiar with the Act – this way, it will become not only a good read, but a good resource).

THE FAIR CREDIT REPORTING ACT

As a public service, the staff of the Federal Trade Commission (FTC) has prepared the following complete text of the Fair Credit Reporting Act (FCRA), 15 U.S.C. § 1681 et seq. Although staff generally followed the format of the U.S. Code as published by the Government Printing Office, the format of this text does differ in minor ways from the Code (and from West's U.S. Code Annotated). For example, this version uses FCRA section numbers (§§ 601-625) in the headings. (The relevant U.S. Code citation is included with each section heading and each reference to the FCRA in the text.)

This version of the FCRA is complete as of January 7, 2002. It includes the amendments to the FCRA set forth in the Consumer Credit Reporting Reform Act of 1996 (Public Law 104-208, the Omnibus Consolidated Appropriations Act for Fiscal Year 1997, Title II, Subtitle D, Chapter 1), Section 311 of the Intelligence Authorization for Fiscal Year 1998 (Public Law 105-107), the Consumer Reporting Employment Clarification Act of 1998 (Public Law 105-347), Section 506 of the Gramm-Leach-Bliley Act (Public Law 106-102), and Sections 358(g) and 505(c) of the Uniting and Strengthening America by Providing Appropriate Tools Required to Intercept and Obstruct Terrorism Act of 2001 (USA PATRIOT Act) (Public Law 107-56).

TABLE OF CONTENTS

§ 601. Short title

This title may be cited as the Fair Credit Reporting Act.

§ 602. Congressional findings and statement of purpose [15 U.S.C. § 1681]

(a) Accuracy and fairness of credit reporting. The Congress makes the following findings:

> (1) The banking system is dependent upon fair and accurate credit reporting. Inaccurate credit reports directly impair the efficiency of the banking system, and unfair credit reporting methods undermine the public confidence which is essential to the continued functioning of the banking system.

> (2) An elaborate mechanism has been developed for investigating and evaluating the credit worthiness, credit standing, credit capacity, character, and general reputation of consumers.

> (3) Consumer reporting agencies have assumed a vital role in assembling and evaluating consumer credit and other information on consumers.

> (4) There is a need to insure that consumer reporting agencies exercise their grave responsibilities with fairness, impartiality, and a respect for the consumer's right to privacy.

(b) Reasonable procedures. It is the purpose of this title to require that consumer reporting agencies adopt reasonable procedures for meeting the needs of commerce for consumer credit, personnel, insurance, and other information in a manner which is fair and equitable to the consumer, with regard to the confidentiality, accuracy, relevancy, and proper utilization of such information in accordance with the requirements of this title.

§ 603. Definitions; rules of construction [15 U.S.C. § 1681a]

(a) Definitions and rules of construction set forth in this section are applicable for the purposes of this title.

(b) The term "person" means any individual, partnership, corporation, trust, estate, cooperative, association, government or governmental subdivision or agency, or other entity.

(c) The term "consumer" means an individual.

(d) Consumer report.

> (1) In general. The term "consumer report" means any written, oral, or other communication of any information by a consumer reporting agency bearing on a consumer's credit worthiness, credit standing, credit capacity, character, general reputation, personal characteristics, or mode of living which is used or expected to be used or collected in whole or in part for the purpose of serving as a factor in establishing the consumer's eligibility for

> (A) credit or insurance to be used primarily for personal, family, or household purposes;

> (B) employment purposes; or

> (C) any other purpose authorized under section 604 [§ 1681b].

> (2) Exclusions. The term "consumer report" does not include

(A) any

(i) report containing information solely as to transactions or experiences between the consumer and the person making the report;

(ii) communication of that information among persons related by common ownership or affiliated by corporate control; or

(iii) communication of other information among persons related by common ownership or affiliated by corporate control, if it is clearly and conspicuously disclosed to the consumer that the information may be communicated among such persons and the consumer is given the opportunity, before the time that the information is initially communicated, to direct that such information not be communicated among such persons;

(B) any authorization or approval of a specific extension of credit directly or indirectly by the issuer of a credit card or similar device;

(C) any report in which a person who has been requested by a third party to make a specific extension of credit directly or indirectly to a consumer conveys his or her decision with respect to such request, if the third party advises the consumer of the name and address of the person to whom the request was made, and such person makes the disclosures to the consumer required under section 615 [§ 1681m]; or

(D) a communication described in subsection (o).

(e) The term "investigative consumer report" means a consumer report or portion thereof in which information on a consumer's character, general reputation, personal characteristics, or mode of living is obtained through personal interviews with neighbors, friends, or associates of the consumer reported on or with others with whom he is acquainted or who may have knowledge concerning any such items of information. However, such information shall not include specific factual information on a consumer's credit record obtained directly from a creditor of the consumer or from a consumer reporting agency when such information was obtained directly from a creditor of the consumer or from the consumer.

(f) The term "consumer reporting agency" means any person which, for monetary fees, dues, or on a cooperative nonprofit basis, regularly engages in whole or in part in the practice of assembling or evaluating consumer credit information or other information on consumers for the purpose of furnishing consumer reports to third parties, and which uses any means or facility of interstate commerce for the purpose of preparing or furnishing consumer reports.

(g) The term "file," when used in connection with information on any consumer, means all of the information on that consumer recorded and retained by a consumer reporting agency regardless of how the information is stored.

(h) The term "employment purposes" when used in connection with a consumer report means a report used for the purpose of evaluating a consumer for employment, promotion, reassignment or retention as an employee.

(i) The term "medical information" means information or records obtained, with the consent of the individual to whom it relates, from licensed physicians or medical practitioners, hospitals, clinics, or other medical or medically related facilities.

(j) Definitions relating to child support obligations.

> (1) Overdue support. The term "overdue support" has the meaning given to such term in section 666(e) of title 42 [Social Security Act, 42 U.S.C. § 666(e)].

> (2) State or local child support enforcement agency. The term "State or local child support enforcement agency" means a State or local agency which administers a State or local program for establishing and enforcing child support obligations.

(k) Adverse action.

> (1) Actions included. The term "adverse action"

> (A) has the same meaning as in section 701(d)(6) of the Equal Credit Opportunity Act; and

> (B) means

> (i) a denial or cancellation of, an increase in any charge for, or a reduction or other adverse or unfavorable change in the terms of coverage or amount of, any insurance, existing or applied for, in connection with the underwriting of insurance;

> (ii) a denial of employment or any other decision for employment purposes that adversely affects any current or prospective employee;

> (iii) a denial or cancellation of, an increase in any charge for, or any other adverse or unfavorable change in the terms of, any license or benefit described in section 604(a)(3)(D) [§ 1681b]; and

> (iv) an action taken or determination that is

> (I) made in connection with an application that was made by, or a transaction that was initiated by, any consumer, or in connection with a review of an account under section 604(a)(3)(F)(ii)[§ 1681b]; and

> (II) adverse to the interests of the consumer.

> (2) Applicable findings, decisions, commentary, and orders. For purposes of any determination of whether an action is an adverse action under paragraph (1)(A), all appropriate final findings, decisions, commentary, and orders issued under section 701(d)(6) of the Equal Credit Opportunity Act by the Board of Governors of the Federal Reserve System or any court shall apply.

(l) Firm offer of credit or insurance. The term "firm offer of credit or insurance" means any offer of credit or insurance to a consumer that will be honored if the consumer is determined, based on information in a consumer report on the consumer, to meet the specific criteria used to select the consumer for the offer, except that the offer may be further conditioned on one or more of the following:

> (1) The consumer being determined, based on information in the consumer's application for the credit or insurance, to meet specific criteria bearing on credit worthiness or insurability, as applicable, that are established

(A) before selection of the consumer for the offer; and

(B) for the purpose of determining whether to extend credit or insurance pursuant to the offer.

(2) Verification

(A) that the consumer continues to meet the specific criteria used to select the consumer for the offer, by using information in a consumer report on the consumer, information in the consumer's application for the credit or insurance, or other information bearing on the credit worthiness or insurability of the consumer; or

(B) of the information in the consumer's application for the credit or insurance, to determine that the consumer meets the specific criteria bearing on credit worthiness or insurability.

(3) The consumer furnishing any collateral that is a requirement for the extension of the credit or insurance that was

(A) established before selection of the consumer for the offer of credit or insurance; and

(B) disclosed to the consumer in the offer of credit or insurance.

(m) Credit or insurance transaction that is not initiated by the consumer. The term"credit or insurance transaction that is not initiated by the consumer" does not include the use of a consumer report by a person with which the consumer has an account or insurance policy, for purposes of

(1) reviewing the account or insurance policy; or

(2) collecting the account.

(n) State. The term "State" means any State, the Commonwealth of Puerto Rico, the District of Columbia, and any territory or possession of the United States.

(o) Excluded communications. A communication is described in this subsection if it is a communication

(1) that, but for subsection (d)(2)(D), would be an investigative consumer report;

(2) that is made to a prospective employer for the purpose of

(A) procuring an employee for the employer; or

(B) procuring an opportunity for a natural person to work for the employer;

(3) that is made by a person who regularly performs such procurement;

(4) that is not used by any person for any purpose other than a purpose described in subparagraph (A) or (B) of paragraph (2); and

(5) with respect to which

(A) the consumer who is the subject of the communication

(i) consents orally or in writing to the nature and scope of the communication, before the collection of any information for the purpose of making the communication;

(ii) consents orally or in writing to the making of the communication to a prospective employer, before the making of the communication; and

(iii) in the case of consent under clause (i) or (ii) given orally, is provided written confirmation of that consent by the person making the communication, not later than 3 business days after the receipt of the consent by that person;

(B) the person who makes the communication does not, for the purpose of making the communication, make any inquiry that if made by a prospective employer of the consumer who is the subject of the communication would violate any applicable Federal or State equal employment opportunity law or regulation; and

(C) the person who makes the communication

(i) discloses in writing to the consumer who is the subject of the communication, not later than 5 business days after receiving any request from the consumer for such disclosure, the nature and substance of all information in the consumer's file at the time of the request, except that the sources of any information that is acquired solely for use in making the communication and is actually used for no other purpose, need not be disclosed other than under appropriate discovery procedures in any court of competent jurisdiction in which an action is brought; and

(ii) notifies the consumer who is the subject of the communication, in writing, of the consumer's right to request the information described in clause (i).

(p) Consumer reporting agency that compiles and maintains files on consumers on a nationwide basis. The term "consumer reporting agency that compiles and maintains files on consumers on a nationwide basis" means a consumer reporting agency that regularly engages in the practice of assembling or evaluating, and maintaining, for the purpose of furnishing consumer reports to third parties bearing on a consumer's credit worthiness, credit standing, or credit capacity, each of the following regarding consumers residing nationwide:

(1) Public record information.

(2) Credit account information from persons who furnish that information regularly and in the ordinary course of business.

§ 604. Permissible purposes of consumer reports [15 U.S.C. § 1681b]

(a) In general. Subject to subsection (c), any consumer reporting agency may furnish a consumer report under the following circumstances and no other:

(1) In response to the order of a court having jurisdiction to issue such an order, or a subpoena issued in connection with proceedings before a Federal grand jury.

(2) In accordance with the written instructions of the consumer to whom it relates.
(3) To a person which it has reason to believe

(A) intends to use the information in connection with a credit transaction involving the consumer on whom the information is to be furnished and involving the extension of credit to, or review or collection of an account of, the consumer; or

(B) intends to use the information for employment purposes; or

(C) intends to use the information in connection with the underwriting of insurance involving the consumer; or

(D) intends to use the information in connection with a determination of the consumer's eligibility for a license or other benefit granted by a governmental instrumentality required by law to consider an applicant's financial responsibility or status; or

(E) intends to use the information, as a potential investor or servicer, or current insurer, in connection with a valuation of, or an assessment of the credit or prepayment risks associated with, an existing credit obligation; or

(F) otherwise has a legitimate business need for the information

(i) in connection with a business transaction that is initiated by the consumer; or

(ii) to review an account to determine whether the consumer continues to meet the terms of the account.

(4) In response to a request by the head of a State or local child support enforcement agency (or a State or local government official authorized by the head of such an agency), if the person making the request certifies to the consumer reporting agency that

(A) the consumer report is needed for the purpose of establishing an individual's capacity to make child support payments or determining the appropriate level of such payments;

(B) the paternity of the consumer for the child to which the obligation relates has been established or acknowledged by the consumer in accordance with State laws under which the obligation arises (if required by those laws);

(C) the person has provided at least 10 days' prior notice to the consumer whose report is requested, by certified or registered mail to the last known address of the consumer, that the report will be requested; and

(D) the consumer report will be kept confidential, will be used solely for a purpose described in subparagraph (A), and will not be used in connection with any other civil, administrative, or criminal proceeding, or for any other purpose.

(5) To an agency administering a State plan under Section 454 of the Social Security Act (42 U.S.C. § 654) for use to set an initial or modified child support award.

(b) Conditions for furnishing and using consumer reports for employment purposes.

(1) Certification from user. A consumer reporting agency may furnish a consumer report for employment purposes only if

(A) the person who obtains such report from the agency certifies to the agency that

(i) the person has complied with paragraph (2) with respect to the consumer report, and the person will comply with paragraph (3) with respect to the consumer report if paragraph (3) becomes applicable; and

(ii) information from the consumer report will not be used in violation of any applicable Federal or State equal employment opportunity law or regulation; and

(B) the consumer reporting agency provides with the report, or has previously provided, a summary of the consumer's rights under this title, as prescribed by the Federal Trade Commission under section 609(c)(3) [§ 1681g].

(2) Disclosure to consumer.

(A) In general. Except as provided in subparagraph (B), a person may not procure a consumer report, or cause a consumer report to be procured, for employment purposes with respect to any consumer, unless--

(i) a clear and conspicuous disclosure has been made in writing to the consumer at any time before the report is procured or caused to be procured, in a document that consists solely of the disclosure, that a consumer report may be obtained for employment purposes; and

(ii) the consumer has authorized in writing (which authorization may be made on the document referred to in clause (i)) the procurement of the report by that person.

(B) Application by mail, telephone, computer, or other similar means. If a consumer described in subparagraph (C) applies for employment by mail, telephone, computer, or other similar means, at any time before a consumer report is procured or caused to be procured in connection with that application--

(i) the person who procures the consumer report on the consumer for employment purposes shall provide to the consumer, by oral, written, or electronic means, notice that a consumer report may be obtained for employment purposes, and a summary of the consumer's rights under section 615(a)(3); and

(ii) the consumer shall have consented, orally, in writing, or electronically to the procurement of the report by that person.

(C) Scope. Subparagraph (B) shall apply to a person procuring a consumer report on a consumer in connection with the consumer's application for employment only if--

(i) the consumer is applying for a position over which the Secretary of Transportation has the power to establish qualifications and maximum hours of service pursuant to the provisions of section 31502 of title 49, or a position subject to safety regulation by a State transportation agency; and

(ii) as of the time at which the person procures the report or causes the report to be procured the only interaction between the consumer and the person in connection with that employment application has been by mail, telephone, computer, or other similar means.

(3) Conditions on use for adverse actions.

(A) In general. Except as provided in subparagraph (B), in using a consumer report for employment purposes, before taking any adverse action based in whole or in part on the report, the person intending to take such adverse action shall provide to the consumer to whom the report relates--

(i) a copy of the report; and

(ii) a description in writing of the rights of the consumer under this title, as prescribed by the Federal Trade Commission under section 609(c)(3).

(B) Application by mail, telephone, computer, or other similar means.

(i) If a consumer described in subparagraph (C) applies for employment by mail, telephone, computer, or other similar means, and if a person who has procured a consumer report on the consumer for employment purposes takes adverse action on the employment application based in whole or in part on the report, then the person must provide to the consumer to whom the report relates, in lieu of the notices required under subparagraph (A) of this section and under section 615(a), within 3 business days of taking such action, an oral, written or electronic notification--

(I) that adverse action has been taken based in whole or in part on a consumer report received from a consumer reporting agency;

(II) of the name, address and telephone number of the consumer reporting agency that furnished the consumer report (including a toll-free telephone number established by the agency if the agency compiles and maintains files on consumers on a nationwide basis);

(III) that the consumer reporting agency did not make the decision to take the adverse action and is unable to provide to the consumer the specific reasons why the adverse action was taken; and

(IV) that the consumer may, upon providing proper identification, request a free copy of a report and may dispute with the consumer reporting agency the accuracy or completeness of any information in a report.

(ii) If, under clause (B)(i)(IV), the consumer requests a copy of a consumer report from the person who procured the report, then, within 3 business days of receiving the consumer's request, together with proper identification, the person must send or provide to the consumer a copy of a report and a copy of the consumer's rights as prescribed by the Federal Trade Commission under section 609(c)(3).

(C) Scope. Subparagraph (B) shall apply to a person procuring a consumer report on a consumer in connection with the consumer's application for employment only if--

(i) the consumer is applying for a position over which the Secretary of Transportation has the power to establish qualifications and maximum hours of service pursuant to the provisions of section 31502 of title 49, or a position subject to safety regulation by a State transportation agency; and

(ii) as of the time at which the person procures the report or causes the report to be procured the only interaction between the consumer and the person in connection with that employment application has been by mail, telephone, computer, or other similar means.

(4) Exception for national security investigations.

(A) In general. In the case of an agency or department of the United States Government which seeks to obtain and use a consumer report for employment purposes, paragraph (3) shall not apply to any adverse action by such agency or department which is based in part on such consumer report, if the head of such agency or department makes a written finding that--

(i) the consumer report is relevant to a national security investigation of such agency or department;

(ii) the investigation is within the jurisdiction of such agency or department;

(iii) there is reason to believe that compliance with paragraph (3) will--

(I) endanger the life or physical safety of any person;

(II) result in flight from prosecution;

(III) result in the destruction of, or tampering with, evidence relevant to the investigation;

(IV) result in the intimidation of a potential witness relevant to the investigation;

(V) result in the compromise of classified information; or

(VI) otherwise seriously jeopardize or unduly delay the investigation or another official proceeding.

(B) Notification of consumer upon conclusion of investigation. Upon the conclusion of a national security investigation described in subparagraph (A), or upon the determination that the exception under subparagraph (A) is no longer required for the reasons set forth in such subparagraph, the official exercising the authority in such subparagraph shall provide to the consumer who is the subject of the consumer report with regard to which such finding was made--

(i) a copy of such consumer report with any classified information redacted as necessary;

(ii) notice of any adverse action which is based, in part, on the consumer report; and

(iii) the identification with reasonable specificity of the nature of the investigation for which the consumer report was sought.

(C) Delegation by head of agency or department. For purposes of subparagraphs (A) and (B), the head of any agency or department of the United States Government may delegate his or her authorities under this paragraph to an official of such agency or department who has personnel security responsibilities and is a member of the Senior Executive Service or equivalent civilian or military rank.

(D) Report to the congress. Not later than January 31 of each year, the head of each agency and department of the United States Government that exercised authority under this paragraph during the preceding year shall submit a report to the Congress on the number of times the department or agency exercised such authority during the year.

(E) Definitions. For purposes of this paragraph, the following definitions shall apply:

(i) Classified information. The term `classified information' means information that is protected from unauthorized disclosure under Executive Order No. 12958 or successor orders.

(ii) National security investigation. The term `national security investigation' means any official inquiry by an agency or department of the United States Government to determine the eligibility of a consumer to receive access or continued access to classified information or to determine whether classified information has been lost or compromised.

(c) Furnishing reports in connection with credit or insurance transactions that are not initiated by the consumer.

(1) In general. A consumer reporting agency may furnish a consumer report relating to any consumer pursuant to subparagraph (A) or (C) of subsection (a)(3) in connection with any credit or insurance transaction that is not initiated by the consumer only if

(A) the consumer authorizes the agency to provide such report to such person; or

(B) (i) the transaction consists of a firm offer of credit or insurance;

(ii) the consumer reporting agency has complied with subsection (e); and

(iii) there is not in effect an election by the consumer, made in accordance with subsection (e), to have the consumer's name and address excluded from lists of names provided by the agency pursuant to this paragraph.

(2) Limits on information received under paragraph (1)(B). A person may receive pursuant to paragraph (1)(B) only

(A) the name and address of a consumer;

(B) an identifier that is not unique to the consumer and that is used by the person solely for the purpose of verifying the identity of the consumer; and

(C) other information pertaining to a consumer that does not identify the relationship or experience of the consumer with respect to a particular creditor or other entity.

(3) Information regarding inquiries. Except as provided in section 609(a)(5) [§ 1681g], a consumer reporting agency shall not furnish to any person a record of inquiries in connection with a credit or insurance transaction that is not initiated by a consumer.

(d) Reserved.

(e) Election of consumer to be excluded from lists.

(1) In general. A consumer may elect to have the consumer's name and address excluded from any list provided by a consumer reporting agency under subsection (c)(1)(B) in connection with a credit or insurance transaction that is not initiated by the consumer, by notifying the agency in accordance with paragraph (2) that the consumer does not consent to any use of a consumer report relating to the consumer in connection with any credit or insurance transaction that is not initiated by the consumer.

(2) Manner of notification. A consumer shall notify a consumer reporting agency under paragraph (1)

(A) through the notification system maintained by the agency under paragraph (5); or

(B) by submitting to the agency a signed notice of election form issued by the agency for purposes of this subparagraph.

(3) Response of agency after notification through system. Upon receipt of notification of the election of a consumer under paragraph (1) through the notification system maintained by the agency under paragraph (5), a consumer reporting agency shall

(A) inform the consumer that the election is effective only for the 2-year period following the election if the consumer does not submit to the agency a signed notice of election form issued by the agency for purposes of paragraph (2)(B); and

(B) provide to the consumer a notice of election form, if requested by the consumer, not later than 5 business days after receipt of the notification of the election through the system established under paragraph (5), in the case of a request made at the time the consumer provides notification through the system.

(4) Effectiveness of election. An election of a consumer under paragraph (1)

(A) shall be effective with respect to a consumer reporting agency beginning 5 business days after the date on which the consumer notifies the agency in accordance with paragraph (2);

(B) shall be effective with respect to a consumer reporting agency

(i) subject to subparagraph (C), during the 2-year period beginning 5 business days after the date on which the consumer notifies the agency of the election, in the case of an election for which a consumer notifies the agency only in accordance with paragraph (2)(A); or

(ii) until the consumer notifies the agency under subparagraph (C), in the case of an election for which a consumer notifies the agency in accordance with paragraph (2)(B);

(C) shall not be effective after the date on which the consumer notifies the agency, through the notification system established by the agency under paragraph (5), that the election is no longer effective; and

(D) shall be effective with respect to each affiliate of the agency.

(5) Notification system.

(A) In general. Each consumer reporting agency that, under subsection (c)(1)(B), furnishes a consumer report in connection with a credit or insurance transaction that is not initiated by a consumer, shall

(i) establish and maintain a notification system, including a toll-free telephone number, which permits any consumer whose consumer report is maintained by the agency to notify the agency, with appropriate identification, of the consumer's election to have the consumer's name and address excluded from any such list of names and addresses provided by the agency for such a transaction; and

(ii) publish by not later than 365 days after the date of enactment of the Consumer Credit Reporting Reform Act of 1996, and not less than annually thereafter, in a publication of general circulation in the area served by the agency

(I) a notification that information in consumer files maintained by the agency may be used in connection with such transactions; and

(II) the address and toll-free telephone number for consumers to use to notify the agency of the consumer's election under clause (I).

(B) Establishment and maintenance as compliance. Establishment and maintenance of a notification system (including a toll-free telephone number) and publication by a consumer reporting agency on the agency's own behalf and on behalf of any of its affiliates in accordance with this paragraph is deemed to be compliance with this paragraph by each of those affiliates.

(6) Notification system by agencies that operate nationwide. Each consumer reporting agency that compiles and maintains files on consumers on a nationwide basis shall establish and maintain a notification system for purposes of paragraph (5) jointly with other such consumer reporting agencies.

(f) Certain use or obtaining of information prohibited. A person shall not use or obtain a consumer report for any purpose unless

(1) the consumer report is obtained for a purpose for which the consumer report is authorized to be furnished under this section; and

(2) the purpose is certified in accordance with section 607 [§ 1681e] by a prospective user of the report through a general or specific certification.

(g) Furnishing reports containing medical information. A consumer reporting agency shall not furnish for employment purposes, or in connection with a credit or insurance transaction, a consumer report that contains medical information about a consumer, unless the consumer consents to the furnishing of the report.

§ 605. Requirements relating to information contained in consumer reports [15 U.S.C. § 1681c]

(a) Information excluded from consumer reports. Except as authorized under subsection (b) of this section, no consumer reporting agency may make any consumer report containing any of the following items of information:

(1) Cases under title 11 [United States Code] or under the Bankruptcy Act that, from the date of entry of the order for relief or the date of adjudication, as the case may be, antedate the report by more than 10 years.

(2) Civil suits, civil judgments, and records of arrest that from date of entry, antedate the report by more than seven years or until the governing statute of limitations has expired, whichever is the longer period.

(3) Paid tax liens which, from date of payment, antedate the report by more than seven years.

(4) Accounts placed for collection or charged to profit and loss which antedate the report by more than seven years.[1]

(5) Any other adverse item of information, other than records of convictions of crimes which antedates the report by more than seven years.[1]

(b) Exempted cases. The provisions of subsection (a) of this section are not applicable in the case of any consumer credit report to be used in connection with

(1) a credit transaction involving, or which may reasonably be expected to involve, a principal amount of $150,000 or more;

(2) the underwriting of life insurance involving, or which may reasonably be expected to involve, a face amount of $150,000 or more; or

(3) the employment of any individual at an annual salary which equals, or which may reasonably be expected to equal $75,000, or more.

(c) Running of reporting period.

(1) In general. The 7-year period referred to in paragraphs (4) and (6)[2] of subsection (a) shall begin, with respect to any delinquent account that is placed for collection (internally or by referral to a third party, whichever is earlier), charged to profit and loss, or subjected to any similar action, upon the expiration of the 180-day period beginning on the date of the commencement of the delinquency which immediately preceded the collection activity, charge to profit and loss, or similar action.

(2) Effective date. Paragraph (1) shall apply only to items of information added to the file of a consumer on or after the date that is 455 days after the date of enactment of the Consumer Credit Reporting Reform Act of 1996.

(d) Information required to be disclosed. Any consumer reporting agency that furnishes a consumer report that contains information regarding any case involving the consumer that arises under title 11, United States Code, shall include in the report an identification of the chapter of such title 11 under which such case arises if provided by the source of the information. If any case arising or filed under title 11, United States Code, is withdrawn by the consumer before a final judgment, the consumer reporting agency shall include in the report that such case or filing was withdrawn upon receipt of documentation certifying such withdrawal.

(e) Indication of closure of account by consumer. If a consumer reporting agency is notified pursuant to section 623(a)(4) [§ 1681s-2] that a credit account of a consumer was voluntarily closed by the consumer, the agency shall indicate that fact in any consumer report that includes information related to the account.

(f) Indication of dispute by consumer. If a consumer reporting agency is notified pursuant to section 623(a)(3) [§ 1681s-2] that information regarding a consumer who was furnished to the agency is disputed by the consumer, the agency shall indicate that fact in each consumer report that includes the disputed information.

§ 606. Disclosure of investigative consumer reports [15 U.S.C. § 1681d]

(a) Disclosure of fact of preparation. A person may not procure or cause to be prepared an investigative consumer report on any consumer unless

(1) it is clearly and accurately disclosed to the consumer that an investigative consumer report including information as to his character, general reputation, personal characteristics and mode of living, whichever are applicable, may be made, and such disclosure

(A) is made in a writing mailed, or otherwise delivered, to the consumer, not later than three days after the date on which the report was first requested, and

(B) includes a statement informing the consumer of his right to request the additional disclosures provided for under subsection (b) of this section and the written summary of the rights of the consumer prepared pursuant to section 609(c) [§ 1681g]; and

(2) the person certifies or has certified to the consumer reporting agency that

(A) the person has made the disclosures to the consumer required by paragraph (1); and
(B) the person will comply with subsection (b).

(b) Disclosure on request of nature and scope of investigation. Any person who procures or causes to be prepared an investigative consumer report on any consumer shall, upon written request made by the consumer within a reasonable period of time after the receipt by him of the disclosure required by subsection (a)(1) of this section, make a complete and accurate disclosure of the nature and scope of the investigation requested. This disclosure shall be made in a writing mailed, or otherwise delivered, to the consumer not later than five days after the date on which the request for such disclosure was received from the consumer or such report was first requested, whichever is the later.

(c) Limitation on liability upon showing of reasonable procedures for compliance with provisions. No person may be held liable for any violation of subsection (a) or (b) of this section if he shows by a preponderance of the evidence that at the time of the violation he maintained reasonable procedures to assure compliance with subsection (a) or (b) of this section.

(d) Prohibitions.

(1) Certification. A consumer reporting agency shall not prepare or furnish investigative consumer report unless the agency has received a certification under subsection (a)(2) from the person who requested the report.
(2) Inquiries. A consumer reporting agency shall not make an inquiry for the purpose of preparing an investigative consumer report on a consumer for employment purposes if the making of the inquiry by an employer or prospective employer of the consumer would violate any applicable Federal or State equal employment opportunity law or regulation.

(3) Certain public record information. Except as otherwise provided in section 613 [§ 1681k], a consumer reporting agency shall not furnish an investigative consumer report that includes information that is a matter of public record and that relates to an arrest, indictment, conviction, civil judicial action, tax lien, or outstanding judgment, unless the agency has verified the accuracy of the information during the 30-day period ending on the date on which the report is furnished.

(4) Certain adverse information. A consumer reporting agency shall not prepare or furnish an investigative consumer report on a consumer that contains information that is adverse to the interest of the consumer and that is obtained through a personal interview with a neighbor, friend, or associate of the consumer or with another person with whom the consumer is acquainted or who has knowledge of such item of information, unless

(A) the agency has followed reasonable procedures to obtain confirmation of the information, from an additional source that has independent and direct knowledge of the information; or

(B) the person interviewed is the best possible source of the information.

§ 607. Compliance procedures [15 U.S.C. § 1681e]

(a) Identity and purposes of credit users. Every consumer reporting agency shall maintain reasonable procedures designed to avoid violations of section 605 [§ 1681c] and to limit the furnishing of consumer reports to the purposes listed under section 604 [§ 1681b] of this title. These procedures shall require that prospective users of the information identify themselves, certify the purposes for which the information is sought, and certify that the information will be used for no other purpose. Every consumer reporting agency shall make a reasonable effort to verify the identity of a new prospective user and the uses certified by such prospective user prior to furnishing such user a consumer report. No consumer reporting agency may furnish a consumer report to any person if it has reasonable grounds for believing that the consumer report will not be used for a purpose listed in section 604 [§ 1681b] of this title.

(b) Accuracy of report. Whenever a consumer reporting agency prepares a consumer report it shall follow reasonable procedures to assure maximum possible accuracy of the information concerning the individual about whom the report relates.

(c) Disclosure of consumer reports by users allowed. A consumer reporting agency may not prohibit a user of a consumer report furnished by the agency on a consumer from disclosing the contents of the report to the consumer, if adverse action against the consumer has been taken by the user based in whole or in part on the report.

(d) Notice to users and furnishers of information.

(1) Notice requirement. A consumer reporting agency shall provide to any person

(A) who regularly and in the ordinary course of business furnishes information to the agency with respect to any consumer; or

(B) to whom a consumer report is provided by the agency;

a notice of such person's responsibilities under this title.

(2) Content of notice. The Federal Trade Commission shall prescribe the content of notices under paragraph (1), and a consumer reporting agency shall be in compliance

with this subsection if it provides a notice under paragraph (1) that is substantially similar to the Federal Trade Commission prescription under this paragraph.

(e) Procurement of consumer report for resale.

(1) Disclosure. A person may not procure a consumer report for purposes of reselling the report (or any information in the report) unless the person discloses to the consumer reporting agency that originally furnishes the report

(A) the identity of the end-user of the report (or information); and

(B) each permissible purpose under section 604 [§ 1681b] for which the report is furnished to the end-user of the report (or information).

(2) Responsibilities of procurers for resale. A person who procures a consumer report for purposes of reselling the report (or any information in the report) shall

(A) establish and comply with reasonable procedures designed to ensure that the report (or information) is resold by the person only for a purpose for which the report may be furnished under section 604 [§ 1681b], including by requiring that each person to which the report (or information) is resold and that resells or provides the report (or information) to any other person

(i) identifies each end user of the resold report (or information);

(ii) certifies each purpose for which the report (or information) will be used; and

(iii) certifies that the report (or information) will be used for no other purpose; and

(B) before reselling the report, make reasonable efforts to verify the identifications and certifications made under subparagraph (A).

(3) Resale of consumer report to a federal agency or department. Notwithstanding paragraph (1) or (2), a person who procures a consumer report for purposes of reselling the report (or any information in the report) shall not disclose the identity of the end-user of the report under paragraph (1) or (2) if--

(A) the end user is an agency or department of the United States Government which procures the report from the person for purposes of determining the eligibility of the consumer concerned to receive access or continued access to classified information (as defined in section 604(b)(4)(E)(i)); and

(B) the agency or department certifies in writing to the person reselling the report that nondisclosure is necessary to protect classified information or the safety of persons employed by or contracting with, or undergoing investigation for work or contracting with the agency or department.

§ 608. Disclosures to governmental agencies [15 U.S.C. § 1681f]

Notwithstanding the provisions of section 604 [§ 1681b] of this title, a consumer reporting agency may furnish identifying information respecting any consumer, limited to his name, address, former addresses, places of employment, or former places of employment, to a governmental agency.

§ 609. Disclosures to consumers [15 U.S.C. § 1681g]

(a) Information on file; sources; report recipients. Every consumer reporting agency shall, upon request, and subject to 610(a)(1) [§ 1681h], clearly and accurately disclose to the consumer:

> (1) All information in the consumer's file at the time of the request, except that nothing in this paragraph shall be construed to require a consumer reporting agency to disclose to a consumer any information concerning credit scores or any other risk scores or predictors relating to the consumer.

> (2) The sources of the information; except that the sources of information acquired solely for use in preparing an investigative consumer report and actually used for no other purpose need not be disclosed: Provided, That in the event an action is brought under this title, such sources shall be available to the plaintiff under appropriate discovery procedures in the court in which the action is brought.

> (3)(A) Identification of each person (including each end-user identified under section 607(e)(1) [§ 1681e]) that procured a consumer report

> (i) for employment purposes, during the 2-year period preceding the date on which the request is made; or

> (ii) for any other purpose, during the 1-year period preceding the date on which the request is made.

> (B) An identification of a person under subparagraph (A) shall include

> (i) the name of the person or, if applicable, the trade name (written in full) under which such person conducts business; and

> (ii) upon request of the consumer, the address and telephone number of the person.

> (C) Subparagraph (A) does not apply if--

> (i) the end user is an agency or department of the United States Government that procures the report from the person for purposes of determining the eligibility of the consumer to whom the report relates to receive access or continued access to classified information (as defined in section 604(b)(4)(E)(i)); and

> (ii) the head of the agency or department makes a written finding as prescribed under section 604(b)(4)(A).

> (4) The dates, original payees, and amounts of any checks upon which is based any adverse characterization of the consumer, included in the file at the time of the disclosure.

> (5) A record of all inquiries received by the agency during the 1-year period preceding the request that identified the consumer in connection with a credit or insurance transaction that was not initiated by the consumer.

(b) Exempt information. The requirements of subsection (a) of this section respecting the disclosure of sources of information and the recipients of consumer reports do not apply to information received or consumer reports furnished prior to the effective date of this title except to the extent that the matter involved is contained in the files of the consumer reporting agency on that date.

(c) Summary of rights required to be included with disclosure.

(1) Summary of rights. A consumer reporting agency shall provide to a consumer, with each written disclosure by the agency to the consumer under this section

(A) a written summary of all of the rights that the consumer has under this title; and

(B) in the case of a consumer reporting agency that compiles and maintains files on consumers on a nationwide basis, a toll-free telephone number established by the agency, at which personnel are accessible to consumers during normal business hours.

(2) Specific items required to be included. The summary of rights required under paragraph (1) shall include

(A) a brief description of this title and all rights of consumers under this title;

(B) an explanation of how the consumer may exercise the rights of the consumer under this title;

(C) a list of all Federal agencies responsible for enforcing any provision of this title and the address and any appropriate phone number of each such agency, in a form that will assist the consumer in selecting the appropriate agency;

(D) a statement that the consumer may have additional rights under State law and that the consumer may wish to contact a State or local consumer protection agency or a State attorney general to learn of those rights; and

(E) a statement that a consumer reporting agency is not required to remove accurate derogatory information from a consumer's file, unless the information is outdated under section 605 [§ 1681c] or cannot be verified.

(3) Form of summary of rights. For purposes of this subsection and any disclosure by a consumer reporting agency required under this title with respect to consumers' rights, the Federal Trade Commission (after consultation with each Federal agency referred to in section 621(b) [§ 1681s]) shall prescribe the form and content of any such disclosure of the rights of consumers required under this title. A consumer reporting agency shall be in compliance with this subsection if it provides disclosures under paragraph (1) that are substantially similar to the Federal Trade Commission prescription under this paragraph.

(4) Effectiveness. No disclosures shall be required under this subsection until the date on which the Federal Trade Commission prescribes the form and content of such disclosures under paragraph (3).

§ 610. Conditions and form of disclosure to consumers [15 U.S.C. § 1681h]

(a) In general.

(1) Proper identification. A consumer reporting agency shall require, as a condition of making the disclosures required under section 609 [§ 1681g], that the consumer furnish proper identification.

(2) Disclosure in writing. Except as provided in subsection (b), the disclosures required to be made under section 609 [§ 1681g] shall be provided under that section in writing.

(b) Other forms of disclosure.

(1) In general. If authorized by a consumer, a consumer reporting agency may make the disclosures required under 609 [§ 1681g]

(A) other than in writing; and

(B) in such form as may be

(i) specified by the consumer in accordance with paragraph (2); and

(ii) available from the agency.

(2) Form. A consumer may specify pursuant to paragraph (1) that disclosures under section 609 [§ 1681g] shall be made

(A) in person, upon the appearance of the consumer at the place of business of the consumer reporting agency where disclosures are regularly provided, during normal business hours, and on reasonable notice;

(B) by telephone, if the consumer has made a written request for disclosure by telephone;

(C) by electronic means, if available from the agency; or

(D) by any other reasonable means that is available from the agency.

(c) Trained personnel. Any consumer reporting agency shall provide trained personnel to explain to the consumer any information furnished to him pursuant to section 609 [§ 1681g] of this title.

(d) Persons accompanying consumer. The consumer shall be permitted to be accompanied by one other person of his choosing, who shall furnish reasonable identification. A consumer reporting agency may require the consumer to furnish a written statement granting permission to the consumer reporting agency to discuss the consumer's file in such person's presence.

(e) Limitation of liability. Except as provided in sections 616 and 617 [§§ 1681n and 1681o] of this title, no consumer may bring any action or proceeding in the nature of defamation, invasion of privacy, or negligence with respect to the reporting of information against any consumer reporting agency, any user of information, or any person who furnishes information to a consumer reporting agency, based on information disclosed pursuant to section 609, 610, or 615 [§§ 1681g, 1681h, or 1681m] of this title or based on information disclosed by a user of a consumer report to or for a consumer against whom the user has taken adverse action, based in whole or in part on the report, except as to false information furnished with malice or willful intent to injure such consumer.

§ 611. Procedure in case of disputed accuracy [15 U.S.C. § 1681i]

(a) Reinvestigations of disputed information.

(1) Reinvestigation required.

(A) In general. If the completeness or accuracy of any item of information contained in a consumer's file at a consumer reporting agency is disputed by the consumer and the consumer notifies the agency directly of such dispute, the agency shall reinvestigate free of charge and record the current status of the disputed information, or delete the item from the file in accordance with paragraph (5), before the end of the 30-day period beginning on the date on which the agency receives the notice of the dispute from the consumer.

(B) Extension of period to reinvestigate. Except as provided in subparagraph (C), the 30-day period described in subparagraph (A) may be extended for not more than 15 additional days if the consumer reporting agency receives information from the consumer during that 30-day period that is relevant to the reinvestigation.

(C) Limitations on extension of period to reinvestigate. Subparagraph (B) shall not apply to any reinvestigation in which, during the 30-day period described in subparagraph (A), the information that is the subject of the reinvestigation is found to be inaccurate or incomplete or the consumer reporting agency determines that the information cannot be verified.

(2) Prompt notice of dispute to furnisher of information.

(A) In general. Before the expiration of the 5-business-day period beginning on the date on which a consumer reporting agency receives notice of a dispute from any consumer in accordance with paragraph (1), the agency shall provide notification of the dispute to any person who provided any item of information in dispute, at the address and in the manner established with the person. The notice shall include all relevant information regarding the dispute that the agency has received from the consumer.

(B) Provision of other information from consumer. The consumer reporting agency shall promptly provide to the person who provided the information in dispute all relevant information regarding the dispute that is received by the agency from the consumer after the period referred to in subparagraph (A) and before the end of the period referred to in paragraph (1)(A).

(3) Determination that dispute is frivolous or irrelevant.

(A) In general. Notwithstanding paragraph (1), a consumer reporting agency may terminate a reinvestigation of information disputed by a consumer under that paragraph if the agency reasonably determines that the dispute by the consumer is frivolous or irrelevant, including by reason of a failure by a consumer to provide sufficient information to investigate the disputed information.

(B) Notice of determination. Upon making any determination in accordance with subparagraph (A) that a dispute is frivolous or irrelevant, a consumer reporting agency shall notify the consumer of such determination not later than 5 business days after making such determination, by mail or, if authorized by the consumer for that purpose, by any other means available to the agency.

(C) Contents of notice. A notice under subparagraph (B) shall include

(i) the reasons for the determination under subparagraph (A); and

(ii) identification of any information required to investigate the disputed information, which may consist of a standardized form describing the general nature of such information.

(4) Consideration of consumer information. In conducting any reinvestigation under paragraph (1) with respect to disputed information in the file of any consumer, the consumer reporting agency shall review and consider all relevant information submitted by the consumer in the period described in paragraph (1)(A) with respect to such disputed information.

(5) Treatment of inaccurate or unverifiable information.

(A) In general. If, after any reinvestigation under paragraph (1) of any information disputed by a consumer, an item of the information is found to be inaccurate or incomplete or cannot be verified, the consumer reporting agency shall promptly delete that item of information from the consumer's file or modify that item of information, as appropriate, based on the results of the reinvestigation.

(B) Requirements relating to reinsertion of previously deleted material.

(i) Certification of accuracy of information. If any information is deleted from a consumer's file pursuant to subparagraph (A), the information may not be reinserted in the file by the consumer reporting agency unless the person who furnishes the information certifies that the information is complete and accurate.

(ii) Notice to consumer. If any information that has been deleted from a consumer's file pursuant to subparagraph (A) is reinserted in the file, the consumer reporting agency shall notify the consumer of the reinsertion in writing not later than 5 business days after the reinsertion or, if authorized by the consumer for that purpose, by any other means available to the agency.

(iii) Additional information. As part of, or in addition to, the notice under clause (ii), a consumer reporting agency shall provide to a consumer in writing not later than 5 business days after the date of the reinsertion

(I) a statement that the disputed information has been reinserted;
(II) the business name and address of any furnisher of information contacted and the telephone number of such furnisher, if reasonably available, or of any furnisher of information that contacted the consumer reporting agency, in connection with the reinsertion of such information; and

(III) a notice that the consumer has the right to add a statement to the consumer's file disputing the accuracy or completeness of the disputed information.

C) Procedures to prevent reappearance. A consumer reporting agency shall maintain reasonable procedures designed to prevent the reappearance in a consumer's file, and in consumer reports on the consumer, of information that is deleted pursuant to this paragraph (other than information that is reinserted in accordance with subparagraph (B)(i)).

D) Automated reinvestigation system. Any consumer reporting agency that compiles and maintains files on consumers on a nationwide basis shall implement an automated system through which furnishers of information to that consumer reporting agency may report the results of a reinvestigation that finds incomplete or inaccurate information in a consumer's file to other such consumer reporting agencies.

(6) Notice of results of reinvestigation.

(A) In general. A consumer reporting agency shall provide written notice to a consumer of the results of a reinvestigation under this subsection not later than 5 business days after the completion of the reinvestigation, by mail or, if authorized by the consumer for that purpose, by other means available to the agency.

(B) Contents. As part of, or in addition to, the notice under subparagraph (A), a consumer reporting agency shall provide to a consumer in writing before the expiration of the 5-day period referred to in subparagraph (A)

(i) a statement that the reinvestigation is completed;

(ii) a consumer report that is based upon the consumer's file as that file is revised as a result of the reinvestigation;

(iii) a notice that, if requested by the consumer, a description of the procedure used to determine the accuracy and completeness of the information shall be provided to the consumer by the agency, including the business name and address of any furnisher of information contacted in connection with such information and the telephone number of such furnisher, if reasonably available;

(iv) a notice that the consumer has the right to add a statement to the consumer's file disputing the accuracy or completeness of the information; and

(v) a notice that the consumer has the right to request under subsection (d) that the consumer reporting agency furnish notifications under that subsection.

(7) Description of reinvestigation procedure. A consumer reporting agency shall provide to a consumer a description referred to in paragraph (6)(B)(iii) by not later than 15 days after receiving a request from the consumer for that description.

(8) Expedited dispute resolution. If a dispute regarding an item of information in a consumer's file at a consumer reporting agency is resolved in accordance with paragraph (5)(A) by the deletion of the disputed information by not later than 3 business days after the date on which the agency receives notice of the dispute from the consumer in accordance with paragraph (1)(A), then the agency shall not be required to comply with paragraphs (2), (6), and (7) with respect to that dispute if the agency

(A) provides prompt notice of the deletion to the consumer by telephone;
(B) includes in that notice, or in a written notice that accompanies a confirmation and consumer report provided in accordance with subparagraph (C), a statement of the consumer's right to request under subsection (d) that the agency furnish notifications under that subsection; and

(C) provides written confirmation of the deletion and a copy of a consumer report on the consumer that is based on the consumer's file after the deletion, not later than 5 business days after making the deletion.

(b) Statement of dispute. If the reinvestigation does not resolve the dispute, the consumer may file a brief statement setting forth the nature of the dispute. The consumer reporting agency may limit such statements to not more than one hundred words if it provides the consumer with assistance in writing a clear summary of the dispute.

(c) Notification of consumer dispute in subsequent consumer reports. Whenever a statement of a dispute is filed, unless there is reasonable grounds to believe that it is frivolous or irrelevant, the consumer reporting agency shall, in any subsequent consumer report containing the information in question, clearly note that it is disputed by the consumer and provide either the consumer's statement or a clear and accurate codification or summary thereof.

(d) Notification of deletion of disputed information. Following any deletion of information which is found to be inaccurate or whose accuracy can no longer be verified or any notation as to disputed information, the consumer reporting agency shall, at the request of the consumer, furnish notification that the item has been deleted or the statement, codification or summary pursuant to subsection (b) or (c) of this section to any person specifically designated by the consumer who has within two years prior thereto received a consumer report for employment purposes, or within six months prior thereto received a consumer report for any other purpose, which contained the deleted or disputed information.

§ 612. Charges for certain disclosures [15 U.S.C. § 1681j]

(a) Reasonable charges allowed for certain disclosures.

(1) In general. Except as provided in subsections (b), (c), and (d), a consumer reporting agency may impose a reasonable charge on a consumer

(A) for making a disclosure to the consumer pursuant to section 609 [§ 1681g], which charge

(i) shall not exceed $8;[3] and

(ii) shall be indicated to the consumer before making the disclosure; and

(B) for furnishing, pursuant to 611(d) [§ 1681i], following a reinvestigation under section 611(a) [§ 1681i], a statement, codification, or summary to a person designated by the consumer under that section after the 30-day period beginning on the date of notification of the consumer under paragraph (6) or (8) of section 611(a) [§ 1681i] with respect to the reinvestigation, which charge

(i) shall not exceed the charge that the agency would impose on each designated recipient for a consumer report; and

(ii) shall be indicated to the consumer before furnishing such information.

(2) Modification of amount. The Federal Trade Commission shall increase the amount referred to in paragraph (1)(A)(I) on January 1 of each year, based proportionally on changes in the Consumer Price Index, with fractional changes rounded to the nearest fifty cents.

(b) Free disclosure after adverse notice to consumer. Each consumer reporting agency that maintains a file on a consumer shall make all disclosures pursuant to section 609 [§ 1681g] without charge to the consumer if, not later than 60 days after receipt by such consumer of a notification pursuant to section 615 [§ 1681m], or of a notification from a debt collection agency affiliated with that consumer reporting agency stating that the consumer's credit rating may be or has been adversely affected, the consumer makes a request under section 609 [§ 1681g].

(c) Free disclosure under certain other circumstances. Upon the request of the consumer, a consumer reporting agency shall make all disclosures pursuant to section 609 [§ 1681g] once during any 12-month period without charge to that consumer if the consumer certifies in writing that the consumer

(1) is unemployed and intends to apply for employment in the 60-day period beginning on the date on which the certification is made;

(2) is a recipient of public welfare assistance; or

(3) has reason to believe that the file on the consumer at the agency contains inaccurate information due to fraud.

(d) Other charges prohibited. A consumer reporting agency shall not impose any charge on a consumer for providing any notification required by this title or making any disclosure required by this title, except as authorized by subsection (a).

§ 613. Public record information for employment purposes [15 U.S.C. § 1681k]

(a) In general. A consumer reporting agency which furnishes a consumer report for employment purposes and which for that purpose compiles and reports items of information on consumers which are matters of public record and are likely to have an adverse effect upon a consumer's ability to obtain employment shall

(1) at the time such public record information is reported to the user of such consumer report, notify the consumer of the fact that public record information is being reported by the consumer reporting agency, together with the name and address of the person to whom such information is being reported; or

(2) maintain strict procedures designed to insure that whenever public record information which is likely to have an adverse effect on a consumer's ability to obtain employment is reported it is complete and up to date. For purposes of this paragraph, items of public record relating to arrests, indictments, convictions, suits, tax liens, and outstanding judgments shall be considered up to date if the current public record status of the item at the time of the report is reported.

(b) Exemption for national security investigations. Subsection (a) does not apply in the case of an agency or department of the United States Government that seeks to obtain and use a consumer report for employment purposes, if the head of the agency or department makes a written finding as prescribed under section 604(b)(4)(A).

§ 614. Restrictions on investigative consumer reports [15 U.S.C. § 1681l]

Whenever a consumer reporting agency prepares an investigative consumer report, no adverse information in the consumer report (other than information which is a matter of public record) may be included in a subsequent consumer report unless such adverse information has been verified in the process of making such subsequent consumer report, or the adverse information was received within the three-month period preceding the date the subsequent report is furnished.

§ 615. Requirements on users of consumer reports [15 U.S.C. § 1681m]

(a) Duties of users taking adverse actions on the basis of information contained in consumer reports. If any person takes any adverse action with respect to any consumer that is based in whole or in part on any information contained in a consumer report, the person shall

(1) provide oral, written, or electronic notice of the adverse action to the consumer;

(2) provide to the consumer orally, in writing, or electronically

(A) the name, address, and telephone number of the consumer reporting agency (including a toll-free telephone number established by the agency if the agency compiles and maintains files on consumers on a nationwide basis) that furnished the report to the person; and

(B) a statement that the consumer reporting agency did not make the decision to take the adverse action and is unable to provide the consumer the specific reasons why the adverse action was taken; and

(3) provide to the consumer an oral, written, or electronic notice of the consumer's right

(A) to obtain, under section 612 [§ 1681j], a free copy of a consumer report on the consumer from the consumer reporting agency referred to in paragraph (2), which notice shall include an indication of the 60-day period under that section for obtaining such a copy; and

(B) to dispute, under section 611 [§ 1681i], with a consumer reporting agency the accuracy or completeness of any information in a consumer report furnished by the agency.

(b) Adverse action based on information obtained from third parties other than consumer reporting agencies.

(1) In general. Whenever credit for personal, family, or household purposes involving a consumer is denied or the charge for such credit is increased either wholly or partly because of information obtained from a person other than a consumer reporting agency bearing upon the consumer's credit worthiness, credit standing, credit capacity, character, general reputation, personal characteristics, or mode of living, the user of such information shall, within a reasonable period of time, upon the consumer's written request for the reasons for such adverse action received within sixty days after learning of such adverse action, disclose the nature of the information to the consumer. The user of such information shall clearly and accurately disclose to the consumer his right to make such written request at the time such adverse action is communicated to the consumer.
(2) Duties of person taking certain actions based on information provided by affiliate.

(A) Duties, generally. If a person takes an action described in subparagraph (B) with respect to a consumer, based in whole or in part on information described in subparagraph (C), the person shall

(i) notify the consumer of the action, including a statement that the consumer may obtain the information in accordance with clause (ii); and

(ii) upon a written request from the consumer received within 60 days after transmittal of the notice required by clause (I), disclose to the consumer the nature of the information upon which the action is based by not later than 30 days after receipt of the request.

(B) Action described. An action referred to in subparagraph (A) is an adverse action described in section 603(k)(1)(A) [§ 1681a], taken in connection with a transaction initiated by the consumer, or any adverse action described in clause (i) or (ii) of section 603(k)(1)(B) [§ 1681a].

(C) Information described. Information referred to in subparagraph (A)

(i) except as provided in clause (ii), is information that

(I) is furnished to the person taking the action by a person related by common ownership or affiliated by common corporate control to the person taking the action; and

(II) bears on the credit worthiness, credit standing, credit capacity, character, general reputation, personal characteristics, or mode of living of the consumer; and

(ii) does not include
(I) information solely as to transactions or experiences between the consumer and the person furnishing the information; or

(II) information in a consumer report.

(c) Reasonable procedures to assure compliance. No person shall be held liable for any violation of this section if he shows by a preponderance of the evidence that at the time of the alleged violation he maintained reasonable procedures to assure compliance with the provisions of this section.

(d) Duties of users making written credit or insurance solicitations on the basis of information contained in consumer files.

(1) In general. Any person who uses a consumer report on any consumer in connection with any credit or insurance transaction that is not initiated by the consumer, that is provided to that person under section 604(c)(1)(B) [§ 1681b], shall provide with each written solicitation made to the consumer regarding the transaction a clear and conspicuous statement that

(A) information contained in the consumer's consumer report was used in connection with the transaction;

(B) the consumer received the offer of credit or insurance because the consumer satisfied the criteria for credit worthiness or insurability under which the consumer was selected for the offer;

(C) if applicable, the credit or insurance may not be extended if, after the consumer responds to the offer, the consumer does not meet the criteria used to select the consumer for the offer or any applicable criteria bearing on credit worthiness or insurability or does not furnish any required collateral;

(D) the consumer has a right to prohibit information contained in the consumer's file with any consumer reporting agency from being used in connection with any credit or insurance transaction that is not initiated by the consumer; and

(E) the consumer may exercise the right referred to in subparagraph (D) by notifying a notification system established under section 604(e) [§ 1681b].

(2) Disclosure of address and telephone number. A statement under paragraph (1) shall include the address and toll-free telephone number of the appropriate notification system established under section 604(e) [§ 1681b].

(3) Maintaining criteria on file. A person who makes an offer of credit or insurance to a consumer under a credit or insurance transaction described in paragraph (1) shall maintain on file the criteria used to select the consumer to receive the offer, all criteria bearing on credit worthiness or insurability, as applicable, that are the basis for determining whether or not to extend credit or insurance pursuant to the offer, and any requirement for the furnishing of collateral as a condition of the extension of credit or insurance, until the expiration of the 3-year period beginning on the date on which the offer is made to the consumer.

(4) Authority of federal agencies regarding unfair or deceptive acts or practices not affected. This section is not intended to affect the authority of any Federal or State agency to enforce a prohibition against unfair or deceptive acts or practices, including the making of false or misleading statements in connection with a credit or insurance transaction that is not initiated by the consumer.

§ 616. Civil liability for willful noncompliance [15 U.S.C. § 1681n]

(a) In general. Any person who willfully fails to comply with any requirement imposed under this title with respect to any consumer is liable to that consumer in an amount equal to the sum of

(1)(A) any actual damages sustained by the consumer as a result of the failure or damages of not less than $100 and not more than $1,000; or

(B) in the case of liability of a natural person for obtaining a consumer report under false pretenses or knowingly without a permissible purpose, actual damages sustained by the consumer as a result of the failure or $1,000, whichever is greater;

(2) such amount of punitive damages as the court may allow; and

(3) in the case of any successful action to enforce any liability under this section, the costs of the action together with reasonable attorney's fees as determined by the court.

(b) Civil liability for knowing noncompliance. Any person who obtains a consumer report from a consumer reporting agency under false pretenses or knowingly without a permissible purpose shall be liable to the consumer reporting agency for actual damages sustained by the consumer reporting agency or $1,000, whichever is greater.

(c) Attorney's fees. Upon a finding by the court that an unsuccessful pleading, motion, or other paper filed in connection with an action under this section was filed in bad faith or for purposes of harassment, the court shall award to the prevailing party attorney's fees reasonable in relation to the work expended in responding to the pleading, motion, or other paper.

§ 617. Civil liability for negligent noncompliance [15 U.S.C. § 1681o]

(a) In general. Any person who is negligent in failing to comply with any requirement imposed under this title with respect to any consumer is liable to that consumer in an amount equal to the sum of

(1) any actual damages sustained by the consumer as a result of the failure;

(2) in the case of any successful action to enforce any liability under this section, the costs of the action together with reasonable attorney's fees as determined by the court.

(b) Attorney's fees. On a finding by the court that an unsuccessful pleading, motion, or other paper filed in connection with an action under this section was filed in bad faith or for purposes of harassment, the court shall award to the prevailing party attorney's fees reasonable in relation to the work expended in responding to the pleading, motion, or other paper.

§ 618. Jurisdiction of courts; limitation of actions [15 U.S.C. § 1681p]

An action to enforce any liability created under this title may be brought in any appropriate United States district court without regard to the amount in controversy, or in any other court of competent jurisdiction, within two years from the date on which the liability arises, except that where a defendant has materially and willfully misrepresented any information required under this title to be disclosed to an individual and the information so misrepresented is material to the establishment of the defendant's liability to that individual under this title, the action may be brought at any time within two years after discovery by the individual of the misrepresentation.

§ 619. Obtaining information under false pretenses [15 U.S.C. § 1681q]

Any person who knowingly and willfully obtains information on a consumer from a consumer reporting agency under false pretenses shall be fined under title 18, United States Code, imprisoned for not more than 2 years, or both.

§ 620. Unauthorized disclosures by officers or employees [15 U.S.C. § 1681r]

Any officer or employee of a consumer reporting agency who knowingly and willfully provides information concerning an individual from the agency's files to a person not authorized to receive that information shall be fined under title 18, United States Code, imprisoned for not more than 2 years, or both.

§ 621. Administrative enforcement [15 U.S.C. § 1681s]

(a) (1) Enforcement by Federal Trade Commission. Compliance with the requirements imposed under this title shall be enforced under the Federal Trade Commission Act [15 U.S.C. §§ 41 et seq.] by the Federal Trade Commission with respect to consumer reporting agencies and all other persons subject thereto, except to the extent that enforcement of the requirements imposed under this title is specifically committed to some other government agency under subsection (b) hereof. For the purpose of the exercise by the Federal Trade Commission of its functions and powers under the Federal Trade Commission Act, a violation of any requirement or prohibition imposed under this title shall constitute an unfair or deceptive act or practice in commerce in violation of section 5(a) of the Federal Trade Commission Act [15 U.S.C. § 45(a)] and shall be subject to enforcement by the Federal Trade Commission under section 5(b) thereof [15 U.S.C. § 45(b)] with respect to any consumer reporting agency or person subject to enforcement by the Federal Trade Commission pursuant to this subsection, irrespective of whether that person is engaged in commerce or meets any other jurisdictional tests in the Federal Trade Commission Act. The Federal Trade Commission shall have such procedural, investigative, and enforcement powers, including the power to issue procedural rules in enforcing compliance with the requirements imposed under this title and to require the filing of reports, the production of documents, and the appearance of witnesses as though the applicable terms and conditions of the Federal Trade Commission Act were part of this title. Any person violating any of the provisions of this title shall be subject to the penalties and entitled to the privileges and immunities provided in the Federal Trade Commission Act as though the applicable terms and provisions thereof were part of this title.

(2)(A) In the event of a knowing violation, which constitutes a pattern or practice of violations of this title, the Commission may commence a civil action to recover a civil penalty in a district court of the United States against any person that violates this title. In such action, such person shall be liable for a civil penalty of not more than $2,500 per violation.

(B) In determining the amount of a civil penalty under subparagraph (A), the court shall take into account the degree of culpability, any history of prior such conduct, ability to pay, effect on ability to continue to do business, and such other matters as justice may require.

(3) Notwithstanding paragraph (2), a court may not impose any civil penalty on a person for a violation of section 623(a)(1) [§ 1681s-2] unless the person has been enjoined from committing the violation, or ordered not to commit the violation, in an action or proceeding brought by or on behalf of the Federal Trade Commission, and has violated the injunction or order, and the court may not impose any civil penalty for any violation occurring before the date of the violation of the injunction or order.

(b) Enforcement by other agencies. Compliance with the requirements imposed under this title with respect to consumer reporting agencies, persons who use consumer reports from such agencies, persons who furnish information to such agencies, and users of information that are subject to subsection (d) of section 615 [§ 1681m] shall be enforced under

(1) section 8 of the Federal Deposit Insurance Act [12 U.S.C. § 1818], in the case of

(A) national banks, and Federal branches and Federal agencies of foreign banks, by the Office of the Comptroller of the Currency;

(B) member banks of the Federal Reserve System (other than national banks), branches and agencies of foreign banks (other than Federal branches, Federal agencies, and insured State branches of foreign banks), commercial lending companies owned or controlled by foreign banks, and organizations operating under section 25 or 25(a) [25A] of the Federal Reserve Act [12 U.S.C. §§ 601 et seq., §§ 611 et seq], by the Board of Governors of the Federal Reserve System; and

(C) banks insured by the Federal Deposit Insurance Corporation (other than members of the Federal Reserve System) and insured State branches of foreign banks, by the Board of Directors of the Federal Deposit Insurance Corporation;

(2) section 8 of the Federal Deposit Insurance Act [12 U.S.C. § 1818], by the Director of the Office of Thrift Supervision, in the case of a savings association the deposits of which are insured by the Federal Deposit Insurance Corporation;

(3) the Federal Credit Union Act [12 U.S.C. §§ 1751 et seq.], by the Administrator of the National Credit Union Administration [National Credit Union Administration Board] with respect to any Federal credit union;

(4) subtitle IV of title 49 [49 U.S.C. §§ 10101 et seq.], by the Secretary of Transportation, with respect to all carriers subject to the jurisdiction of the Surface Transportation Board;

(5) the Federal Aviation Act of 1958 [49 U.S.C. Appx §§ 1301 et seq.], by the Secretary of Transportation with respect to any air carrier or foreign air carrier subject to that Act [49 U.S.C. Appx §§ 1301 et seq.]; and

(6) the Packers and Stockyards Act, 1921 [7 U.S.C. §§ 181 et seq.] (except as provided in section 406 of that Act [7 U.S.C. §§ 226 and 227]), by the Secretary of Agriculture with respect to any activities subject to that Act.

The terms used in paragraph (1) that are not defined in this title or otherwise defined in section 3(s) of the Federal Deposit Insurance Act (12 U.S.C. §1813(s)) shall have the meaning given to them in section 1(b) of the International Banking Act of 1978 (12 U.S.C. § 3101).

(c) State action for violations.

(1) Authority of states. In addition to such other remedies as are provided under State law, if the chief law enforcement officer of a State, or an official or agency designated by a State, has reason to believe that any person has violated or is violating this title, the State

(A) may bring an action to enjoin such violation in any appropriate United States district court or in any other court of competent jurisdiction;

(B) subject to paragraph (5), may bring an action on behalf of the residents of the State to recover

(i) damages for which the person is liable to such residents under sections 616 and 617 [§§ 1681n and 1681o] as a result of the violation;

(ii) in the case of a violation of section 623(a) [§ 1681s-2], damages for which the person would, but for section 623(c) [§ 1681s-2], be liable to such residents as a result of the violation; or

(iii) damages of not more than $1,000 for each willful or negligent violation; and

(C) in the case of any successful action under subparagraph (A) or (B), shall be awarded the costs of the action and reasonable attorney fees as determined by the court.

(2) Rights of federal regulators. The State shall serve prior written notice of any action under paragraph (1) upon the Federal Trade Commission or the appropriate Federal regulator determined under subsection (b) and provide the Commission or appropriate Federal regulator with a copy of its complaint, except in any case in which such prior notice is not feasible, in which case the State shall serve such notice immediately upon instituting such action. The Federal Trade Commission or appropriate Federal regulator shall have the right

(A) to intervene in the action;

(B) upon so intervening, to be heard on all matters arising therein;

(C) to remove the action to the appropriate United States district court; and

(D) to file petitions for appeal.

(3) Investigatory powers. For purposes of bringing any action under this subsection, nothing in this subsection shall prevent the chief law enforcement officer, or an official or agency designated by a State, from exercising the powers conferred on the chief law enforcement officer or such official by the laws of such State to conduct investigations or to administer oaths or affirmations or to compel the attendance of witnesses or the production of documentary and other evidence.

(4) Limitation on state action while federal action pending. If the Federal Trade Commission or the appropriate Federal regulator has instituted a civil action or an administrative action under section 8 of the Federal Deposit Insurance Act for a violation of this title, no State may, during the pendency of such action, bring an action under this section against any defendant named in the complaint of the Commission or the appropriate Federal regulator for any violation of this title that is alleged in that complaint.

(5) Limitations on state actions for violation of section 623(a)(1) [§ 1681s-2].

(A) Violation of injunction required. A State may not bring an action against a person under paragraph (1)(B) for a violation of section 623(a)(1) [§ 1681s-2], unless

(i) the person has been enjoined from committing the violation, in an action brought by the State under paragraph (1)(A); and

(ii) the person has violated the injunction.

(B) Limitation on damages recoverable. In an action against a person under paragraph (1)(B) for a violation of section 623(a)(1) [§ 1681s-2], a State may not recover any damages incurred before the date of the violation of an injunction on which the action is based.

(d) Enforcement under other authority. For the purpose of the exercise by any agency referred to in subsection (b) of this section of its powers under any Act referred to in that subsection, a violation of any requirement imposed under this title shall be deemed to be a violation of a requirement imposed under that Act. In addition to its powers under any provision of law specifically referred to in subsection (b) of this section, each of the agencies referred to in that subsection may exercise, for the purpose of enforcing compliance with any requirement imposed under this title any other authority conferred on it by law.

(e) Regulatory authority

(1) The Federal banking agencies referred to in paragraphs (1) and (2) of subsection (b) shall jointly prescribe such regulations as necessary to carry out the purposes of this Act with respect to any persons identified under paragraphs (1) and (2) of subsection (b), and the Board of Governors of the Federal Reserve System shall have authority to prescribe regulations consistent with such joint regulations with respect to bank holding companies and affiliates (other than depository institutions and consumer reporting agencies) of such holding companies.

(2) The Board of the National Credit Union Administration shall prescribe such regulations as necessary to carry out the purposes of this Act with respect to any persons identified under paragraph (3) of subsection (b).

§ 622. Information on overdue child support obligations [15 U.S.C. § 1681s-1]

Notwithstanding any other provision of this title, a consumer reporting agency shall include in any consumer report furnished by the agency in accordance with section 604 [§ 1681b] of this title, any information on the failure of the consumer to pay overdue support which

(1) is provided

(A) to the consumer reporting agency by a State or local child support enforcement agency; or

(B) to the consumer reporting agency and verified by any local, State, or Federal government agency; and

(2) antedates the report by 7 years or less.

§ 623. Responsibilities of furnishers of information to consumer reporting agencies [15 U.S.C. § 1681s-2]

(a) Duty of furnishers of information to provide accurate information.

(1) Prohibition.

(A) Reporting information with actual knowledge of errors. A person shall not furnish any information relating to a consumer to any consumer reporting agency if the person knows or consciously avoids knowing that the information is inaccurate.

(B) Reporting information after notice and confirmation of errors. A person shall not furnish information relating to a consumer to any consumer reporting agency if

(i) the person has been notified by the consumer, at the address specified by the person for such notices, that specific information is inaccurate; and

(ii) the information is, in fact, inaccurate.

(C) No address requirement. A person who clearly and conspicuously specifies to the consumer an address for notices referred to in subparagraph (B) shall not be subject to subparagraph (A); however, nothing in subparagraph (B) shall require a person to specify such an address.

(2) Duty to correct and update information. A person who

(A) regularly and in the ordinary course of business furnishes information to one or more consumer reporting agencies about the person's transactions or experiences with any consumer; and

(B) has furnished to a consumer reporting agency information that the person determines is not complete or accurate, shall promptly notify the consumer reporting agency of that determination and provide to the agency any corrections to that information, or any additional information, that is necessary to make the information provided by the person to the agency complete and accurate, and shall not thereafter furnish to the agency any of the information that remains not complete or accurate.

(3) Duty to provide notice of dispute. If the completeness or accuracy of any information furnished by any person to any consumer reporting agency is disputed to such person by a consumer, the person may not furnish the information to any consumer reporting agency without notice that such information is disputed by the consumer.

(4) Duty to provide notice of closed accounts. A person who regularly and in the ordinary course of business furnishes information to a consumer reporting agency regarding a consumer who has a credit account with that person shall notify the agency of the voluntary closure of the account by the consumer, in information regularly furnished for the period in which the account is closed.

(5) Duty to provide notice of delinquency of accounts. A person who furnishes information to a consumer reporting agency regarding a delinquent account being placed for collection, charged to profit or loss, or subjected to any similar action shall, not later than 90 days after furnishing the information, notify the agency of the month and year of the commencement of the delinquency that immediately preceded the action.

(b) Duties of furnishers of information upon notice of dispute.

(1) In general. After receiving notice pursuant to section 611(a)(2) [§ 1681i] of a dispute with regard to the completeness or accuracy of any information provided by a person to a consumer reporting agency, the person shall

(A) conduct an investigation with respect to the disputed information;

(B) review all relevant information provided by the consumer reporting agency pursuant to section 611(a)(2) [§ 1681i];

(C) report the results of the investigation to the consumer reporting agency; and

(D) if the investigation finds that the information is incomplete or inaccurate, report those results to all other consumer reporting agencies to which the person furnished the information and that compile and maintain files on consumers on a nationwide basis.

(2) Deadline. A person shall complete all investigations, reviews, and reports required under paragraph (1) regarding information provided by the person to a consumer reporting agency, before the expiration of the period under section 611(a)(1) [§ 1681i] within which the consumer reporting agency is required to complete actions required by that section regarding that information.

(c) Limitation on liability. Sections 616 and 617 [§§ 1681n and 1681o] do not apply to any failure to comply with subsection (a), except as provided in section 621(c)(1)(B) [§ 1681s].

(d) Limitation on enforcement. Subsection (a) shall be enforced exclusively under section 621 [§ 1681s] by the Federal agencies and officials and the State officials identified in that section.

§ 624. Relation to State laws [15 U.S.C. § 1681t]

(a) In general. Except as provided in subsections (b) and (c), this title does not annul, alter, affect, or exempt any person subject to the provisions of this title from complying with the laws of any State with respect to the collection, distribution, or use of any information on consumers, except to the extent that those laws are inconsistent with any provision of this title, and then only to the extent of the inconsistency.

(b) General exceptions. No requirement or prohibition may be imposed under the laws of any State

(1) with respect to any subject matter regulated under

(A) subsection (c) or (e) of section 604 [§ 1681b], relating to the prescreening of consumer reports;

(B) section 611 [§ 1681i], relating to the time by which a consumer reporting agency must take any action, including the provision of notification to a consumer or other person, in any procedure related to the disputed accuracy of information in a consumer's file, except that this subparagraph shall not apply to any State law in effect on the date of enactment of the Consumer Credit Reporting Reform Act of 1996;

(C) subsections (a) and (b) of section 615 [§ 1681m], relating to the duties of a person who takes any adverse action with respect to a consumer;

(D) section 615(d) [§ 1681m], relating to the duties of persons who use a consumer report of a consumer in connection with any credit or insurance transaction that is not initiated by the consumer and that consists of a firm offer of credit or insurance;

(E) section 605 [§ 1681c], relating to information contained in consumer reports, except that this subparagraph shall not apply to any State law in effect on the date of enactment of the Consumer Credit Reporting Reform Act of 1996; or

(F) section 623 [§ 1681s-2], relating to the responsibilities of persons who furnish information to consumer reporting agencies, except that this paragraph shall not apply

(i) with respect to section 54A(a) of chapter 93 of the Massachusetts Annotated Laws (as in effect on the date of enactment of the Consumer Credit Reporting Reform Act of 1996); or

(ii) with respect to section 1785.25(a) of the California Civil Code (as in effect on the date of enactment of the Consumer Credit Reporting Reform Act of 1996);

(2) with respect to the exchange of information among persons affiliated by common ownership or common corporate control, except that this paragraph shall not apply with respect to subsection (a) or (c)(1) of section 2480e of title 9, Vermont Statutes Annotated (as in effect on the date of enactment of the Consumer Credit Reporting Reform Act of 1996); or

(3) with respect to the form and content of any disclosure required to be made under section 609(c) [§ 1681g].

(c) Definition of firm offer of credit or insurance. Notwithstanding any definition of the term "firm offer of credit or insurance" (or any equivalent term) under the laws of any State, the definition of that term contained in section 603(*l*) [§ 1681a] shall be construed to apply in the enforcement and interpretation of the laws of any State governing consumer reports.

(d) Limitations. Subsections (b) and (c)

(1) do not affect any settlement, agreement, or consent judgment between any State Attorney General and any consumer reporting agency in effect on the date of enactment of the Consumer Credit Reporting Reform Act of 1996; and

(2) do not apply to any provision of State law (including any provision of a State constitution) that

(A) is enacted after January 1, 2004;

(B) states explicitly that the provision is intended to supplement this title; and

(C) gives greater protection to consumers than is provided under this title.

§ 625. Disclosures to FBI for counterintelligence purposes [15 U.S.C. § 1681u]

(a) Identity of financial institutions. Notwithstanding section 604 [§ 1681b] or any other provision of this title, a consumer reporting agency shall furnish to the Federal Bureau of Investigation the names and addresses of all financial institutions (as that term is defined in section 1101 of the Right to Financial Privacy Act of 1978 [12 U.S.C. § 3401]) at which a consumer maintains or has maintained an account, to the extent that information is in the files of the agency, when presented with a written request for that information, signed by the Director of the Federal Bureau of Investigation, or the Director's designee in a position not lower than Deputy Assistant Director at Bureau headquarters or a Special Agent in Charge of a Bureau field office designated by the Director, which certifies compliance with this section. The Director or the Director's designee may make such a certification only if the Director or the Director's designee has determined in writing, that such information is sought for the conduct of an authorized investigation to protect against international terrorism or clandestine intelligence activities, provided that such an investigation of a United States person is not conducted solely upon the basis of activities protected by the first amendment to the Constitution of the United States.

(b) Identifying information. Notwithstanding the provisions of section 604 [§ 1681b] or any other provision of this title, a consumer reporting agency shall furnish identifying information respecting a consumer, limited to name, address, former addresses, places of employment, or former places of employment, to the Federal Bureau of Investigation when presented with a written request, signed by the Director or the Director's designee, which certifies compliance with this subsection. The Director or the Director's designee in a position not lower than Deputy Assistant Director at Bureau headquarters or a Special Agent in Charge of a Bureau field office designated by the Director may make such a certification only if the Director or the Director's designee has determined in writing that such information is sought for the conduct of an authorized investigation to protect against international terrorism or clandestine intelligence activities, provided that such an investigation of a United States person is not conducted solely upon the basis of activities protected by the first amendment to the Constitution of the United States.

(c) Court order for disclosure of consumer reports. Notwithstanding section 604 [§ 1681b] or any other provision of this title, if requested in writing by the Director of the Federal Bureau of Investigation, or a designee of the Director in a position not lower than Deputy Assistant Director at Bureau headquarters or a Special Agent in Charge of a Bureau field office designated by the Director, a court may issue an order ex parte directing a consumer reporting agency to furnish a consumer report to the Federal Bureau of Investigation, upon a showing in camera that the consumer report is sought for the conduct of an authorized investigation to protect against international terrorism or clandestine intelligence activities, provided that such an investigation of a United States person is not conducted solely upon the basis of activities protected by the first amendment to the Constitution of the United States.

The terms of an order issued under this subsection shall not disclose that the order is issued for purposes of a counterintelligence investigation.

(d) Confidentiality. No consumer reporting agency or officer, employee, or agent of a consumer reporting agency shall disclose to any person, other than those officers, employees, or agents of a consumer reporting agency necessary to fulfill the requirement to disclose information to the Federal Bureau of Investigation under this section, that the Federal Bureau of Investigation has sought or obtained the identity of financial institutions or a consumer report respecting any consumer under subsection (a), (b), or (c), and no consumer reporting agency or officer, employee, or agent of a consumer reporting agency shall include in any consumer report any information that would indicate that the Federal Bureau of Investigation has sought or obtained such information or a consumer report.

(e) Payment of fees. The Federal Bureau of Investigation shall, subject to the availability of appropriations, pay to the consumer reporting agency assembling or providing report or information in accordance with procedures established under this section a fee for reimbursement for such costs as are reasonably necessary and which have been directly incurred in searching, reproducing, or transporting books, papers, records, or other data required or requested to be produced under this section.

(f) Limit on dissemination. The Federal Bureau of Investigation may not disseminate information obtained pursuant to this section outside of the Federal Bureau of Investigation, except to other Federal agencies as may be necessary for the approval or conduct of a foreign counterintelligence investigation, or, where the information concerns a person subject to the Uniform Code of Military Justice, to appropriate investigative authorities within the military department concerned as may be necessary for the conduct of a joint foreign counterintelligence investigation.

(g) Rules of construction. Nothing in this section shall be construed to prohibit information from being furnished by the Federal Bureau of Investigation pursuant to a subpoena or court order, in connection with a judicial or administrative proceeding to enforce the provisions of this Act. Nothing in this section shall be construed to authorize or permit the withholding of information from the Congress.

(h) Reports to Congress. On a semiannual basis, the Attorney General shall fully inform the Permanent Select Committee on Intelligence and the Committee on Banking, Finance and Urban Affairs of the House of Representatives, and the Select Committee on Intelligence and the Committee on Banking, Housing, and Urban Affairs of the Senate concerning all requests made pursuant to subsections (a), (b), and (c).

(i) Damages. Any agency or department of the United States obtaining or disclosing any consumer reports, records, or information contained therein in violation of this section is liable to the consumer to whom such consumer reports, records, or information relate in an amount equal to the sum of

(1) $100, without regard to the volume of consumer reports, records, or information involved;

(2) any actual damages sustained by the consumer as a result of the disclosure;

(3) if the violation is found to have been willful or intentional, such punitive damages as a court may allow; and

(4) in the case of any successful action to enforce liability under this subsection, the costs of the action, together with reasonable attorney fees, as determined by the court.

(j) Disciplinary actions for violations. If a court determines that any agency or department of the United States has violated any provision of this section and the court finds that the circumstances surrounding the violation raise questions of whether or not an officer or employee of the agency or department acted willfully or intentionally with respect to the violation, the agency or department shall promptly initiate a proceeding to determine whether or not disciplinary action is warranted against the officer or employee who was responsible for the violation.

(k) Good-faith exception. Notwithstanding any other provision of this title, any consumer reporting agency or agent or employee thereof making disclosure of consumer reports or identifying information pursuant to this subsection in good-faith reliance upon a certification of the Federal Bureau of Investigation pursuant to provisions of this section shall not be liable to any person for such disclosure under this title, the constitution of any State, or any law or regulation of any State or any political subdivision of any State.

(l) Limitation of remedies. Notwithstanding any other provision of this title, the remedies and sanctions set forth in this section shall be the only judicial remedies and sanctions for violation of this section.

(m) Injunctive relief. In addition to any other remedy contained in this section, injunctive relief shall be available to require compliance with the procedures of this section. In the event of any successful action under this subsection, costs together with reasonable attorney fees, as determined by the court, may be recovered.

§ 626. Disclosures to governmental agencies for counterterrorism purposes [15 U.S.C. §1681v]

(a) Disclosure. Notwithstanding section 604 or any other provision of this title, a consumer reporting agency shall furnish a consumer report of a consumer and all other information in a consumer's file to a government agency authorized to conduct investigations of, or intelligence or counterintelligence activities or analysis related to, international terrorism when presented with a written certification by such government agency that such information is necessary for the agency's conduct or such investigation, activity or analysis.

(b) Form of certification. The certification described in subsection (a) shall be signed by a supervisory official designated by the head of a Federal agency or an officer of a Federal agency whose appointment to office is required to be made by the President, by and with the advice and consent of the Senate.

(c) Confidentiality. No consumer reporting agency, or officer, employee, or agent of such consumer reporting agency, shall disclose to any person, or specify in any consumer report, that a government agency has sought or obtained access to information under subsection (a).

(d) Rule of construction. Nothing in section 625 shall be construed to limit the authority of the Director of the Federal Bureau of Investigation under this section.

(e) Safe harbor. Notwithstanding any other provision of this title, any consumer reporting agency or agent or employee thereof making disclosure of consumer reports or other information pursuant to this section in good-faith reliance upon a certification of a governmental agency pursuant to the provisions of this section shall not be liable to any person for such disclosure under this subchapter, the constitution of any State, or any law or regulation of any State or any political subdivision of any State.

Legislative History

House Reports:
      No. 91-975 (Comm. on Banking and Currency) and
      No. 91-1587 (Comm. of Conference)

Senate Reports:
      No. 91-1139 accompanying S. 3678 (Comm. on Banking and Currency)

Congressional Record, Vol. 116 (1970)
      May 25, considered and passed House.
      Sept. 18, considered and passed Senate, amended.
      Oct. 9, Senate agreed to conference report.
      Oct. 13, House agreed to conference report.

Enactment:
      Public Law No. 91-508 (October 26, 1970):

Amendments: Public Law Nos.
      95-473 (October 17, 1978)
      95-598 (November 6, 1978)
      98-443 (October 4, 1984)
      101-73 (August 9, 1989)
      102-242 (December 19, 1991)
      102-537 (October 27, 1992)
      102-550 (October 28, 1992)
      103-325 (September 23, 1994)
      104-88 (December 29, 1995)
      104-93 (January 6, 1996)
      104-193 (August 22, 1996)
      104-208 (September 30, 1996)
      105-107 (November 20, 1997)
      105-347 (November 2, 1998)
      106-102 (November 12, 1999)
      107-56 (October 26, 2001)

Endnotes:

1. The reporting periods have been lengthened for certain adverse information pertaining to U.S. Government insured or guaranteed student loans, or pertaining to national direct student loans. See sections 430A(f) and 463(c)(3) of the Higher Education Act of 1965, 20 U.S.C. 1080a(f) and 20 U.S.C. 1087cc(c)(3), respectively.

2. Should read "paragraphs (4) and (5)...." Prior Section 605(a)(6) was amended and re-designated as Section 605(a)(5) in November 1998.

3. The Federal Trade Commission increased the maximum allowable charge to $9.00, effective January 1, 2002. 66 Fed. Reg. 63545 (Dec. 7, 2001).

Appendix B

IRS Form 12277

Form **12277**
(October 2011)

Department of the Treasury — Internal Revenue Service

Application for Withdrawal of Filed
Form 668(Y), Notice of Federal Tax Lien
(Internal Revenue Code Section 6323(j))

1. Taxpayer Name *(as shown on the Notice of Federal Tax Lien)*

2. Social Security/Employer Identification No.

3. Taxpayer's Representative, if applicable, or Name and Title of contact person, if taxpayer is a business

4. Address *(Number, Street, P.O. Box)*

5. City

6. State

7. ZIP code

8. Phone Number

9. Attach copy of the Form 668(Y), Notice of Federal Tax Lien, if available, OR, if you don't have a copy, provide the following information, if available:

Serial number of Form 668(Y) *(found near the top of the document)*

Date Form 668(Y) filed

Recording office where Form 668(Y) was filed

10. Current status of the federal tax lien *("x" appropriate box)*

☐ Open   ☐ Released   ☐ Unknown

11. Reason for requesting withdrawal of the filed Notice of Federal Tax Lien *("x" appropriate box(es))*

☐ The Notice of Federal Tax Lien was filed prematurely or not in accordance with IRS procedures.

☐ The taxpayer entered into an installment agreement to satisfy the liability for which the lien was imposed and the agreement did not provide for a Notice of Federal Tax Lien to be filed.

☐ The taxpayer is under a Direct Debit Installment Agreement.

☐ Withdrawal will facilitate collection of the tax.

☐ The taxpayer, or the Taxpayer Advocate acting on behalf of the taxpayer, believes withdrawal is in the best interest of the taxpayer and the government.

12. Explain the basis for the withdrawal request *(attach additional sheets and other documentation that substantiates your request, as needed)*

Affirmation

Under penalties of perjury, I declare that I have examined this application (including any accompanying schedules, exhibits, affidavits, and statements) and, to the best of my knowledge and belief, it is true, correct, and complete

Signature *(Taxpayer or Representative)*

Title *(if business)*

Date

Sources and Resources

As I mentioned at the beginning of this book, I read anything and everything I can find on the subject of credit. Over the years, I have amassed an enormous amount of information from a variety of books, websites, articles, and assorted outlets. The list below is in no way complete, but includes source material for this book and what I consider to be some great resources for additional and more in-depth information.

Books

Detweiler, Gerri. *The Ultimate Credit Handbook: Cut Your Debt and Have a Lifetime of Great Credit.* (January 28, 2003)

Hendricks, Evan. *Credit Scores & Credit Reports: How the System Really Works, What You Can Do.* Privacy Times (May 2004)

McNaughton, Deborah. *The Essential Credit Repair Handbook* Career Press (May 15, 2011)

Rich, Jason R. *Dirty Little Secrets: What the Credit Bureaus Won't Tell You* Entrepreneur Press (July 28, 2006)

Ulzheimer, John. *The Smart Consumer's Guide to Good Credit* Allworth Press (May 1, 2012)

Ventura, John. *The Credit Repair Kit: Everything You Need to Know to Maintain, Rebuild, and Protect Your Credit* Kaplan Business (April 1, 2004)

Weston, Liz Pulliam. *Your Credit Score: How to Improve the 3-Digit Number That Shapes Your*

Financial Future FT Press (October 22, 2015)

Additional Books

Michael Chitwood and Don Meares – *Insider's Tips on Credit Repair – Debt is not your Destiny.*

Jason R. Rich – *Dirty Little Secrets – What the Credit Reporting Agencies Won't Tell You* (2nd Edition) Enterprise Press

John Ventura - *The Credit Repair Handbook* (Third Edition) Dearborn. A Kaplan Professional Company.

Online Resources:

www.myFICO®.com

Federal Trade Commission Consumer Education

My Fico

Identity Theft Resource Center

FICO—Smart Credit Blog

FICO Banking Analytic Blog

Online Articles

Consumer and Credit Reporting, Scoring, and Related Policy Issues by Darryl E. Getter (July 30, 2015). Congressional Research Service.

Consumer Voices on Credit Reports and Scores (February 2015). Consumer Financial Protection Bureau

The impact of differences between consumer and credit purchased credit scores (July 2011). Consumer Financial Protection Bureau

http://files.consumerfinance.gov/f/201212_cfpb_credit-reporting-white-paper.pdf

40 Years of Experience with the Fair Credit Reporting Act: An FTC StaReport with Summary of Interpretations.

The Surprising (and Some Not So Surprising) Credit Habits of the Top 25%

Understand the Impact of Student Loans on Credit Scores By EQUAL JUSTICE WORKS

Research: Millennials Still Seek "Old School" Credit -FICO

IRS Announces New Effort to Help Struggling Taxpayers Get a fresh Start; Major Changes Made to Lien Process

IR-2011-20, Feb. 24, 2011

http://www.irs.gov/uac/IRS-Announces- New- Effort-to-He!p-Struggling-Taxpayers-Get-a-...8/26/2013

Up:*llwww.wsj.com/*articlcs/your-frco,credit·score-actually-there-are many 1435337636

http://www.wsj.com/articles/your-fico-credit-score-actually-there-are-many-J 4353376366/29/2015

http://www.myfico.com/crediteducation/fico-score-versions.aspx6/29/2015

http://www.myfico.com/CreditEducation/FICO-Score-Versions.aspx3/26/2015

http://www.myfico.com/crediteducation/fico-score-versions.aspx6/29/2015

http://www.myfico.com/CreditEducation/FICO-Score-Versions.aspx3/26/2015

http://www.creditsense.com/blog/fico-vs-fake-o-scores-what-is-what/

About The Author

Trent L. Pettus is the Broker and Owner of Integrity Real Estate Services, a full service real estate company licensed in Pennsylvania and Delaware. Over the years, Mr. Pettus has worked in various areas of the real estate industry, including in commercial and residential sales and development, in property management, as a mortgage broker, as a housing and credit counselor, and eventually as the host of "Let's Talk Real Estate" on a radio show in Philadelphia. Currently, Mr. Pettus teaches classes at a local real estate school and serves on the Board of Directors of both the Greater Philadelphia Association of Realtors® (GPAR) and the Pennsylvania Association of Realtors® (PAR). Mr. Pettus is a graduate of North Carolina State University.

www.ingramcontent.com/pod-product-compliance
Lightning Source LLC
Chambersburg PA
CBHW050504210326
41521CB00011B/2322